Cuisine of California

By

THE CALIFORNIA RESTAURANT ASSOCIATION

Marmac Publishing Company, Inc.
Atlanta, Georgia

Copyright© 1984 Marmac Publishing Company, Inc.
6303 Barfield Road, Suite 208, Atlanta, Georgia 30328

ISBN: 0-939944-40-5

Library of Congress Catalog Card Number: 84-070398

Publisher and Executive Editor, Marge McDonald
Senior Editor, Susan Hunter Smith
Recipe Editor, Elise Griffin
Book design by Susan Hunter Smith
Cover photograph by The Crow's Nest Restaurant, Santa Cruz, California

Manufactured in the United States of America

Restaurants featured are members of the California Restaurant Association

CONTENTS

FOREWORD

In a sunny California kitchen, a meal is in progress. How does it all happen? The variety and abundance of flavors, colors, and textures . . . coming together, becoming a memorable meal?

"I wish I had the recipe from that wonderful restaurant we went to . . . if only I knew the chef!"

Well, now you can know the secrets of California chefs. Within the pages of this cookbook are privileged communications from our chefs to you: the secrets of California's great restaurants!

"I never realized it could be so easy. . . why didn't I think of seasoning it that way?"

The ingredients of California cuisine are here, in recipes tested and refined by our best restaurants so you can recreate popular dishes in your own kitchen. Our California chefs lead you step by step through the pleasures and presentations of fine cookery to that climactic:

"So that's how it's done!" and on to those cherished exclamations of your guests:

"How did you do it?"

California cuisine is born of sunshine, adventure, and romance. Californians are as accustomed to variety and contrast in their food and in their restaurants as they are in their farmlands and fruit groves, in their mountains, ocean and deserts, in their new and in their old cultures and communities.

How to define California cuisine? My interpretation is that it's not a thing, but an experience captured in the magic of unexpected combinations, perfected in the tradition of excellence by our great chefs. California cuisine attracts and it welcomes, into the restaurant, or into the home. It's a sharing among friends.

Now, relax with confidence as you share our easy-to-follow recipes. There are no more secrets between friends, between our chefs in their restaurant kitchens and you in yours. And, from our chefs, a very special communication.

"Enjoy!"

Stanley R. Kyker
Executive Vice President
California Restaurant Association

=INTRODUCTION=

The joys of the California dining table are an endlessly varied adventure for all of us who appreciate the art of fine foods and wines. While we may look forward to enjoying many favorite dishes as longtime friends, always comfortable, always a delight, California invites us to venture down unexplored avenues, meet new friends and savor totally unique dining experiences.

FRESH FROM CALIFORNIA

This vast, wondrous Golden State overflows with an astonishing cornucopia of culinary pleasures. Just imagine a world without California's oranges and peaches, unblessed by its avocados, artichokes, apricots, lemons, walnuts and almonds, dates, grapes, vegetables, beef, and fish.

This arsenal of raw materials has been adapted and continuously given new shape by a rich cultural heritage dating back to the 16th century, when Spanish missionaries planted olive and fruit trees along the Camino Real, and produced the first wines from plantings brought from their homeland. The padres were followed by Mexicans, Russians, the gold-seeking 49ers, and by waves of Orientals, who came to labor on the railroads and remained to implant their ancient cultures on the fertile new land.

More recent times have seen surges of Central and South Americans, Europeans, Canadians, hundreds of thousands of newcomers from every corner of Asia, and millions of Americans from every state. Each group has brought something new to California's table.

A CROSS-CULTURAL TOUR

The major magnets of dining California style are Los Angeles and San Francisco. Each of these great metropolitan areas can be a ticket for a culinary tour of the United Nations. Given the time, and sufficient endurance, a food adventurer could joyfully Marco Polo his or her way through Northern and Western Africa, Eastern and Western Europe, the Middle East, the Phillipines, India, Korea, Japan, New Orleans and New England, Guatemala and Argentina, with a domestic tour of the All-American steak and hamburger, without ever applying for a visa or getting on a plane.

These taste-filled tours are also readily available in California's other major cities — sunny San Diego, San Jose, the capital city of Sacramento, picturesque Monterey Peninsula — and in communities from the Mexican border to Oregon, and from the desert to the Pacific.

When the world thinks of dining California style, it often conjures visions of dewey-fresh salads built on a variety of lettuce and adorned with the state's famous avocados, citrus fruits, almonds and walnuts, and perhaps crowned with shrimp, crabmeat, and abalone from a 780-mile-long shoreline. California's plentiful catch from the sea is complemented by salmon, steelhead trout, and other freshwater delicacies from thousands of rivers, streams, lakes, and canals.

With its colorful Mexican history, California has given the spicy food lovers of the world its own special ways with tacos, chile rellenos, green corn tamales, and burritos, whose *picante* flavors are assuaged by frosty pitchers of margaritas.

LAND OF WINES

Like Mexican food without margaritas, no California table would be complete without a selection of our wonderful wines. Eons before Omar Khayyam poetically married a jug of wine with a loaf of bread and thou, the fermented juice of the grape was intimately entwined with the enjoyment of fine foods.

Sun-kissed wines from California's fertile valleys consistently earn the most coveted gold medals for excellence in this country and from the most discriminating wine societies abroad.

Hospitable Californians everywhere invite you to sit at their table and marvel in the fabulous foods and wines of our land. *Bon appetit!*

William Schemmel
Travel Writer

OSTADA COMPUESTA
'l Cholo
age 45

VEAL VENNINI
Alfredo's
Page 51

DOUBLE DECKER CHEESE CAKE
Carmel Butcher Shop
age 93

CHOCOLATE FUDGE TORT
Shadowbrook
Page 91

VOCADO SEAFOOD SALAD
Masterson's Walnut Creek Station
age 32

AURORA PACIFICA
Victor's
Page 100

AYLESBURY DUCKLING
The Cat & the Custard Cup
Page 71

VEAL CARDINAL
The Sardine Factory
Page 49

BLACK BEAN SOUP
Solomon Grundy's
Page 17

BOUILLABAISSE
Hungry Tiger
Page 85

FRESH STRAWBERRY PIE
Hickman's
Page 89

BAKED COUNTRY RABBIT CHASSUERS
Farley's Family Restaurant
Page 57

DEEP-FRIED ICE CREAM
El Torito
Page 103

SAMBOUSAK
Hala Bazaar
Page 15

LINGUINI PESCADORI
The Rogue
Page 59

CAFE MOUSSE
The Crow's Nest
Page 104

ENGLISH TRIFLE
Gulliver's
Page 97

LISA MARIE BURRITO
Barragan's Irish Mexican Cafe
Page 63

BAKED STUFFED SHRIMP
The Spindrifter
Page 77

APPETIZERS
SOUPS

El Cholo

*Town & Country Center, 777 S. Main St.,
Orange, CA 92668;
(714) 972-9900.*

The youngest member of the El Cholo family, the El Cholo in Orange recently celebrated its fourth anniversary. Small, cozy, and handsomely decorated, this delightful dining place offers the same delicious Mexican dishes that have long made its siblings in Los Angeles and La Habra so popular. Diners sit in high-backed wooden booths in a garden room and a small patio that faces Main Street. Favorite dishes include giant burritos, seven vegetable tostados, and puffy chile rellenos.

EL CHOLO GUACAMOLE

10 ripe avocados
½ bunch cilantro, finely chopped
  (see Glossary)
½ white onion, finely chopped
1 (6-ounce) can tomatoes
2 jalapeno peppers, finely
  chopped
1 tablespoon salt
Juice of ½ lemon
1 (3-ounce) can green chiles, finely
  chopped

Peel avocados, remove seed, and mash pulp with fork to form a paste.

Add cilantro, onion, tomatoes, peppers, salt, lemon juice, and chiles and mix until thoroughly blended.

Serve as a dip with tortilla chips or raw vegetables.

MAKES ABOUT 1½ QUARTS

Hala Bazaar

Beverly Center, 8522 Beverly Blvd.,
Los Angeles, CA 90048;
(213) 657-3544.

Hala Bazaar is an exotic Middle Eastern/Mediterranean dining experience that combines two restaurants in one, plus a tempting gourmet grocery displaying spices and freshly-baked pastries. Hala is a full-service restaurant inviting guests to dine on delectable cuisines in a fantasy setting of palm trees, mosque-like arches, and a spacious patio. Bazaar is a unique fast food restaurant, serving the freshest Middle Eastern/Mediterranean specialties to be enjoyed at home.

SAMBOUSAK (A Middle Eastern mezze or appetizer)

Yogurt Dressing
1 medium cucumber
2 cloves garlic, finely chopped
2 cups plain yogurt
1 tablespoon chopped fresh dill
3 tablespoons olive oil
Salt and pepper to taste

Sambousak
3 tablespoons olive oil
3 cloves garlic, finely chopped
2 green onions, finely chopped
1/2 medium onion, finely chopped
1 pound ground lamb
1 teaspoon cumin
Salt and pepper to taste
1 hard boiled egg, finely chopped
1/4 cup finely chopped parsley
1 box phyllo dough (available
   frozen in gourmet shops)
Vegetable oil for frying
1/4 cup sesame seeds

Garnish
4 lemon wedges

To make yogurt dressing: Peel cucumber. Slice in half lengthwise and spoon out all seeds. Place cucumbers and other ingredients, reserving some chopped dill for garnish, in food processor or blender and puree. Chill.

To make sambousak: In skillet heat olive oil over medium heat. Add garlic and onions and saute until onions are transparent, about 5 to 10 minutes. Add lamb, cumin, salt, and pepper. Cook until pinkness is gone from meat.

Set aside to cool. When the mixture is cool, drain off all fat and be certain meat is well broken up. Place meat in mixing bowl. Add hard boiled egg and parsley and mix well.

Place 3 individual sheets of phyllo dough, one on top of the other, on cutting board. Each sheet should measure 12 inches by 14 inches. Cut into strips about 12 inches long and 2 1/2 or 3 inches wide. Be certain dough is not dry and cracking. Keep a moist towel handy and follow directions on package to keep dough pliable.

Place 1 tablespoon of meat mixture onto one end of the phyllo dough strip. Fold the strip to form a triangle by folding the 3-inch end over the mixture to meet the long side. Continue this process alternating the triangle folds at least 3 times. Wet the edge of the last fold with water and press against the triangle puff to secure.

Place vegetable oil, at least 1 inch deep, in frying pan and heat to 360 degrees F. Place sambousaks into oil and brown, about 30 seconds. Drain and sprinkle with sesame seeds. Garnish with lemon wedges and reserved chopped dill and serve with chilled yogurt dressing.

MAKES ABOUT 50 APPETIZERS
Photograph, Page 11

The Danville Hotel Restaurant & Saloon

155 S. Hartz Ave., Danville, CA 94526;
(415) 837-6627.

The Danville Hotel Restaurant and Saloon has been a famous excursion destination since it was built in the late 1800s. As far back as 1937, the legendary Duncan Hines gave the establishment his coveted seal of approval. The hotel's prime rib, seafood, chicken, and gourmet Mexican specialties are famous in this part of California, and many recipes have been published in leading gourmet magazines.

OYSTERS BROCHETTE MONTEBELLO

24 oysters
24 mushroom caps
24 slices bacon, cut in half
1 cup oil
1 teaspoon salt
1 teaspoon dry English mustard
Pinch of pepper
1 cup bread crumbs
1/3 cup butter
2 tablespoons lemon juice
1/2 cup butter, melted

Wrap oysters and mushroom caps separately in bacon and alternate on 4 skewers.

Dip in mixture of oil, salt, mustard, and pepper.

Roll in bread crumbs and saute in skillet in butter over medium heat for 15 minutes, turning to brown all sides.

Combine lemon juice and melted butter and serve as a dipping sauce for oysters.

Note: This recipe is from the Danville Hotel when German chef Paul Zeibig ran the operation in 1937.

MAKES 4 SERVINGS

*100 Seawall Dr., Berkeley, CA 94710;
(415) 548-1876.*

Solomon Grundy's honors its mythical, high-spirited namesake by generating a feeling of comradeship and conviviality. From the moment guests cross Solomon Grundy's bridge and open the massive hand-carved doors, they feel as though they have entered a modern-day castle. Perched above the waters of San Francisco Bay, at Berkeley Marina, the restaurant is a pleasing blend of natural woods, deep earthy colors, fireplaces, and deep comfortable chairs and sofas that invite guests to linger over excellent food and drinks.

GRUNDY'S BLACK BEAN SOUP

*1/2 pound dried black beans
3 quarts plus 3/4 cup water
1 pound smoked ham hocks
1 teaspoon oregano
1 teaspoon garlic powder
1 teaspoon black pepper
1 teaspoon thyme
1/2 teaspoon celery salt
2 bay leaves
2 1/2 ounces sherry
3/4 cup oil
3/4 cup flour*

Garnish
*Lemon slices
Grated hard boiled egg*

Place black beans in a 4-quart kettle with water, ham hocks, oregano, garlic powder, pepper, thyme, celery salt, and bay leaves. Bring to a boil and simmer for 2 hours. Add sherry.

Mix oil and flour together in small bowl. Stir thoroughly and slowly add to the kettle, stirring constantly. Lower heat below simmering point and cook for an additional 15 minutes.

Serve in soup bowls, garnished with a lemon slice and 1 teaspoon grated egg per serving.

MAKES 10 SERVINGS

Photograph, Page 11

571 S. Main St., Orange, CA 92668;
(714) 542-3595.

Chez Cary is like a United Nations in miniature. From Belgium, Switzerland, Austria, France, and Germany, from the U.S., Canada, and Latin America, the restaurant's culinary staff brings together a wealth of traditions and talents to assure an outstanding gourmet experience. The dining room is highlighted by gleaming crystal, flickering candles, and exquisite china. A beautiful setting for a memorable evening.

COLD CUCUMBER SOUP

6 medium cucumbers
1 quart yogurt
1/2 cup sour cream
2 cups half and half
12 fresh mint leaves, finely
   chopped
Dash of Worcestershire sauce
Salt and white pepper to taste
1 tablespoon sugar
Dash of curry powder

Garnish
1 tablespoon chopped chives

Peel cucumbers and slice lengthwise into two halves. Use a spoon and remove all seeds. Slice cucumber halves first the long way into 1/8-inch strips and then 1/8-inch cubes.

In a bowl blend yogurt, sour cream, half and half, mint leaves, Worcestershire, salt, pepper, sugar, and curry powder until smooth and creamy. Stir in chopped cucumbers and chill.

Serve cold in soup cups or plates and sprinkle chopped chives on top.

MAKES 8 SERVINGS

Bank of America World Headquarters Bldg.,
555 California St., San Francisco, CA 94104;
(415) 433-7500.

The Carnelian Room is named for the carnelian color of the Bank of America World Headquarters' granite exterior. Perched 52 stories high and offering a breathtaking view of the city, the bay, and the Pacific Ocean, this remarkable restaurant will treat you to award-winning cuisine and old-world charm. The interior is decorated with remarkable pieces of furniture of the Louis XV and Louis XVI periods, as well as mirrors, consoles, paneling, and paintings by old masters.

ABALONE SOUP

1/2 cup plus 2 tablespoons butter
11/2 cups flour
3 cloves garlic, finely chopped
1 shallot, finely chopped
2 pounds abalone, finely chopped
　(see Glossary)
3 cups clam juice
3 cups fish stock (see Basic Stocks)
1/2 cup white wine
Salt and white pepper to taste
Juice of 1 small lemon
1 tablespoon butter
1/2 cup heavy cream

In large saucepan melt 1/2 cup plus 2 tablespoons butter and add flour to make a roux (see Glossary). Let cook slowly over low heat for 1 to 2 minutes; do not brown. Add garlic, shallots, and 13/4 pounds of the abalone into roux and simmer for 2 minutes.

Heat clam juice and fish stock and add to roux, stirring constantly with a wire whisk. Raise heat and bring to a boil. Reduce heat, add wine, and cook slowly for 10 to 15 minutes. Season to taste with salt and white pepper. Add lemon juice and strain.

Saute remaining 1/4 pound of abalone in 1 tablespoon of butter. Add cream, mix into the strained soup, and serve.

MAKES 8 SERVINGS

Twenty-Six Locations in California.

Hungry Tiger seems to have a monopoly on Maine lobster, since more than 10,000 pounds of this sweet-tasting delicacy are flown into the multiple restaurant locations every month. Along with these tasty Down East favorites, Hungry Tiger specializes in California seafoods, and fish and shellfish from waters all over the world; and many customers come in exclusively for a steaming bowl of Hungry Tiger's famous clam chowder.

CLAM CHOWDER

4 tablespoons butter
1 cup diced onion
1 cup diced leek, white part only
1/3 cup diced celery
1/3 cup diced green pepper
2 tablespoons flour
2 cups water
2 cups bottled clam juice
Salt and white pepper to taste
1 small bay leaf
1/2 teaspoon thyme
2/3 cup potato, peeled and diced
4 tablespoons dry white wine
1 cup chopped clams, drained
1/2 cup warm half and half

Melt butter in large saucepan. Add onion, leek, celery, and green pepper and cook, stiring over medium heat until tender, but not brown.

Lower heat, stir in flour, and cook over very low heat for 2 to 3 minutes. Add water, clam juice, salt, pepper, bay leaf, and thyme. Bring to a boil and add potato and wine.

Cover and simmer 30 minutes or until potatoes are soft.

Add clams and simmer 5 minutes longer. Remove bay leaf and stir in the warm half and half just before serving.

MAKES 6 SERVINGS

Westin St. Francis Hotel, Union Square, 335 Powell St., San Francisco, CA 94102; (415) 774-0233.

A wonderful dining experience at the famed St. Francis, the English Grill is one of downtown San Francisco's very favorite fresh seafood restaurants. Graced with a lovely turn-of-the-century decor, the Grill's tempting selections include a variety of fish and shellfish from California waters, as well as Maine lobster, and other delicacies flown in fresh daily. These dishes are complemented by premium California wines poured by the glass.

ST. FRANCIS CURRIED CLAM CHOWDER

¹/₄ pound bacon, diced
1 cup diced onions
1 clove garlic, chopped
1 cup diced green peppers
1 cup diced celery
³/₄ cup flour
2 tablespoons curry powder
8 tablespoons tomato paste
1 cup clam juice
1 cup fish stock (see Basic Stocks)
Salt and pepper to taste
1 cup diced potatoes
¹/₂ cup diced canned clams
¹/₂ cup heavy cream

Saute together bacon, onions, garlic, green peppers, and celery for 10 minutes.

Stir in flour and curry powder and cook, stirring for 3 minutes. Add tomato paste and mix well.

Add clam juice, fish stock, salt, and pepper and cook for about 20 minutes. Add potatoes and clams and simmer for an additional 30 minutes.

Just before serving, add the cream.

MAKES 6 SERVINGS

3 Embarcadero Center, San Francisco, CA 94111;
(415) 433-7444.

Patterned after the ambiance of an English men's club, Scott's Carriage House welcomes you with plush carpets, big comfortable chairs, and English hunting scenes on the wainscotted walls. The soothing decor of forest green and white with dark wood accents enhances your superb meal of traditional English dishes, grilled meats, and seafood specialties such as calamari and fishermen's stew. At the same address is this restaurant's affiliate, Scott's Seafood Grill & Bar.

SCOTT'S CLAM CHOWDER

3 cups sliced celery
1 cup chopped onions
1/2 teaspoon finely chopped garlic
1 teaspoon thyme
1 teaspoon salt
2 teaspoons white pepper
1 tablespoon butter
1/4 cup dry sherry
5 cups bottled clam juice
4 cups chopped canned clams
5 cups fish stock (see Basic Stocks)
1 pound potatoes, peeled and
    diced
1 cup butter
2 cups flour
3 cups half and half

Combine celery, onions, garlic, thyme, salt, pepper, and 1 tablespoon butter in a heavy pot. Cook over low heat until vegetables are tender. Do not brown.

Add sherry and simmer 2 minutes. Add clam juice, clams, stock, and potatoes. Simmer until potatoes are tender.

Melt 1 cup butter in small, heavy pan. Add flour to make a roux (see Glossary). Stir well to blend and cook over low flame for 10 minutes.

Add roux to chowder and mix well to prevent lumps. Simmer 10 minutes, stirring often. Add half and half just before serving. Heat, but do not boil.

MAKES 16 SERVINGS

The Corkscrew
English Beef and Seafood House

11647 San Vicente Blvd., Los Angeles, CA 90049;
(213) 826-5501

Veteran California restaurant owners Buzz and Mary Helen Dublin have presided over The Corkscrew in Brentwood since 1969. The secrets of their success are many. The atmosphere is warm and comfortable, reminiscent of the rustic public houses of 18th and 19th century England. The Corkscrew's menu offers a wide selection of prime beef, fish, and chicken, prepared in a variety of imaginative ways.

GAZPACHO

2 small cucumbers, peeled
1 (12-ounce) can tomatoes
1 small pimiento
1 clove garlic, minced
2 tablespoons chopped green onion
1/2 green pepper, minced
1 small carrot, minced
1/2 teaspoon salt
2 tablespoons vinegar or lemon juice
1 tablespoon olive oil
1 pinch of sugar
1 pinch of cumin
1 pinch of pepper
1/2 tablespoon paprika
1 1/2 cups water
3/4 cup chilled chicken stock or consomme

Garnish
Croutons
Chopped chives
Chopped hard boiled egg
Cubed fresh tomatoes
Chopped green pepper
Chopped parsley
Chopped celery
Bacon bits
Ground fresh black pepper

In blender coarsely grind cucumbers, tomatoes, pimiento, garlic, onion, peppers, and carrots. Add salt and let stand for several hours.

In separate bowl, combine vinegar or lemon juice, olive oil, sugar, cumin, pepper, and paprika and let stand for 1/2 hour.

Combine both mixtures, add water and chicken stock or consomme, stir all ingredients, and chill in refrigerator for about 2 hours.

Serve in chilled glass cups with garnishes of your choice.

MAKES 4 SERVINGS

Pam Pam East

398 Geary St., San Francisco, CA. 94102;
(415) 433-0113.

A block from Union Square, in the heart of San Francisco's theater, shopping, and hotel district, the warm brick atmosphere of Pam Pam East is an irresistable, around-the-clock magnet for interesting people of all sorts. What's it famous for? Start with Belgian waffles and "hangover" omelettes, go from there to steak soup, stuffed Pacific red snapper, giant tostadas, and hamburgers, and you still haven't begun to cover Pam Pam's numerous specialties. After more than 35 years, it just keeps getting better.

STEAK SOUP

*2 pounds round steak, finely
  chopped*
1/2 cup butter
1 medium onion, finely chopped
1 large carrot, finely chopped
4 ribs celery, finely chopped
1 cup flour
*2 (16-ounce) cans whole tomatoes,
  finely chopped*
*2 quarts consomme or beef stock
  (see Basic Stocks)*
*1 tablespoon monosodium
  glutamate*
Salt and pepper to taste
2 cups half and half

Brown meat in large kettle over moderately high heat. Add butter, onion, carrot, and celery. Stir in flour and cook for 10 minutes.

Add tomatoes, stock, monosodium glutamate, salt, and pepper. Bring to a boil, then lower heat, and simmer for 1 hour. Add half and half about 10 minutes before removing from stove.

This soup can be frozen for later use. If it gets too thick, more beef stock may be added.

MAKES 12 SERVINGS

BREADS · SALADS VEGGIES

Griswold's Indian Hill

555 W. Foothill Blvd.,
Claremont, CA 91711;
(714) 624-9691.

Since opening as a simple roadside stand on Foothill Boulevard in Claremont back in 1950, Griswold's Smorgasbord Restaurants in Claremont and Redlands have grown into a Southern California tradition. Million of customers have sampled the astonishing variety of foods that make up Griswold's smorgasbord table. To keep them coming back, no two smorgasbords are ever alike. Grisword's continental bakeries also attract bread and pastry lovers from across Southern California.

BRAN MUFFINS

Muffin Spread
1/4 cup butter or margarine
6 tablespoons brown sugar
6 tablespoons granulated sugar
2 tablespoons honey
1 tablespoon water

Muffin Batter
1/2 cup whole wheat flour
3/4 cup cake flour
6 tablespoons sugar
1/2 teaspoon salt
1/2 teaspoon cinnamon
1/2 teaspoon baking soda
1/2 cup raisins
2 eggs, lightly beaten
1/4 cup honey
1/4 cup oil
1/4 cup crushed pineapple, drained
3 cups whole bran cereal
1 1/2 cups buttermilk

To make muffin spread: Cream butter in electric mixer. Gradually beat in sugars. Blend in honey and water and whip until fluffy. Coat muffin tins liberally and evenly with mixture, using about 2 teaspoons per tin.

To make muffin batter: Combine flours, sugar, salt, cinnamon, and baking soda in medium bowl. Stir in raisins, eggs, honey, oil, and pineapple. Stir in bran and buttermilk and mix until batter is smooth. Do not overmix.

Fill coated muffin tins three-fourths full. Bake at 400 degrees F. for 18 to 20 minutes. Remove muffins from tins immediately by turning tins upside down onto cooling racks.

MAKES 18 MUFFINS

Mrs. Knott's Chicken Dinner Restaurant

*Knott's Berry Farm, 8039 Beach Blvd.,
Buena Park, CA. 90622;
(714) 827-1776.*

This cheerful, charming dining place began with a need, and an inspiration. Like most Americans in the dark days of the Great Depression, Walter and Cordelia Knott were having difficulty making ends meet. So, they conceived the notion of preparing Cordelia's special chicken dinners for hungry customers. Word spread quickly, and a success was born. Nowadays, even though Knott's Berry Farm is one of America's largest themed amusement parks, Cordelia's chicken dinners haven't changed one delicious bit.

BUTTERMILK BISCUITS

*1¹/₂ cups all purpose flour
2 tablespoons baking powder
Pinch of salt
1 tablespoon shortening
¹/₄ teaspoon baking soda
1 cup buttermilk
Vegetable oil for pans*

In electric mixer, combine flour, baking powder, salt, and shortening and mix until consistency of coarse meal.

In separate bowl combine baking soda and buttermilk and beat with a spoon until foamy and thickened. Add buttermilk mixture to flour and beat until well blended. Do not overbeat. Mixture will be sticky.

Turn out onto well-floured board, sprinkle top of dough with flour, and pat until 1 inch thick.

Pour enough (about ¹/₄ cup) oil into jelly roll pan (approximately 11 inches by 7 inches). Oil should fill pans to ¹/₄ inch. In second pan pour an equal amount of oil.

Cut biscuits with cookie cutter, roll each biscuit in the first pan of oil, and then place in second pan. Oil will cling to dough, which is desirable. Continue cutting and rolling in oil until second pan is filled. Biscuits should be touching each other. Pat top of biscuits with oil from first pan.

Bake at 500 degrees F. for 10 to 12 minutes or until golden brown.

MAKES APPROXIMATELY 18 TWO-INCH BISCUITS

19643 E. Avenue "P", Palmdale, CA 93550; (805) 264-2169.

In 1974 Richard and Jeanne Blalock went against the advice of their many friends, and took over an existing restaurant in the Antelope Valley that had failed. Happily, the Blalocks quickly proved the wisdom of their move. In 1981, Mr. B's had become so popular that it had to be doubled in size. The addition includes a superb wine cellar, featuring over 215 selections from California and Europe. The menu includes steaks, rack of lamb, and fresh seafoods. "Mr. B" himself plays the piano in the lounge for weekend dancing.

PUMPKIN BREAD

2 cups sugar
1/3 cup water
1 cup plus 2 tablespoons corn oil
6 eggs
1 teaspoon vanilla extract
1 (16-ounce) can pumpkin
4 3/4 cups all purpose flour
1 teaspoon nutmeg
1 teaspoon cinnamon
1/8 teaspoon salt
1 teaspoon baking soda
1 teaspoon baking powder
1/2 pound chopped walnuts
1/2 cup raisins
Flour for dusting

Place sugar, water, corn oil, eggs, vanilla extract, and pumpkin in large bowl of electric mixer. Beat at low speed to combine.

Sift flour, nutmeg, cinnamon, salt, baking soda, and baking powder together and add gradually to egg mixture to combine.

Lightly dust walnuts and raisins with flour and add to mixture.

Pour into 6 well greased 4 1/2-inch by 2 3/4-inch by 2-inch loaf pans, filling a little more than half full. Bake at 350 degrees F. for 1 hour or until done. Remove from pans and cool on rack.

MAKES 6 INDIVIDUAL LOAVES

Eureka, CA 95501; (707) 442-1659.
Call for directions.

In a landmark building over 100 years old, Samoa Cookhouse is one of the last surviving lumber camp cookhouses in the United States. Sit down at the big long table and eat your fill of hearty American food the same way lumberjacks did a century ago. Surrounded by artifacts such as pots and pans, axes and chainsaws (there's even a museum off the main dining room), you'll be served a complete meal in traditional cookhouse style. There's no menu to select from (except at dinner, when there are two choices of entrees). Bring your own wine or beer if you wish.

SAMOA COOKHOUSE PANCAKES

7 eggs
1/2 cup vegetable oil
1/3 tablespoon salt
1 teaspoon vanilla extract
1/8 teaspoon yellow food
  coloring
2 cups all purpose flour
1 3/4 cup cake flour
1/2 cup sugar
1 teaspoon baking soda
2 tablespoons baking powder
1 quart buttermilk

In mixing bowl combine eggs, vegetable oil, salt, vanilla, and food coloring. Mix lightly at medium speed.

Sift flours, sugar, baking soda, and baking powder together. Add alternately with buttermilk, using mixer on low speed. Mix well but do not overmix.

To cook, pour 1/4 cup batter onto greased griddle and cook until bubbles appear on surface. Turn to brown other side. Remove to warm oven until all pancakes are cooked.

MAKES 6 TO 8 SERVINGS

Locations all over California.

During the early 1920s, an ambitious young Iowan named W.W. Naylor came West and opened the first Tiny's Waffle Shop. Known to everyone as "Tiny", Naylor's concept of family restaurants serving only top quality ingredients at modest prices caught on very quickly. Today, a new generation still runs Tiny's in the sound, old-fashioned way, and Californians enjoy bakery products, chili, waffles, cream pies, hamburgers, and other tasty foods from the San Fernando Valley to San Juan Capistrano.

EVERYDAY WAFFLES

*1³/₄ cups sifted all purpose flour
or 2 cups sifted cake flour
1 tablespoon baking powder
¹/₂ teaspoon salt
2 eggs, separated
1¹/₄ cups milk (or equal parts
evaporated milk and water)
¹/₄ cup melted shortening or
salad oil*

Sift flour, baking powder, and salt together into medium bowl.

In another bowl, beat egg yolks and add milk and shortening, mixing well. Combine with dry ingredients.

Beat egg whites until stiff, but not dry, and fold into batter.

Pour batter into hot waffle iron. Waffles are done when steam is no longer visible.

MAKES 6 WAFFLES

Francois'

Arco Plaza, 555 S. Flower St., C Level,
Los Angeles, CA 90071;
(213) 680-2727.

The award-winning Francois' is one of Los Angeles' most distinctive restaurants. The management has combined the elegance of a beautifully appointed dining room with memorable cuisine and personalized service. Over the past decade, Francois' has been "the" place for a smart early dinner for patrons of the nearby Music Center and the Hollywood Bowl and Greek Theatre. Francois' menu offers an extensive selection of fresh seafood, veal, lamb, steak, frogs legs, and many more classical dishes.

SALADE FRANCOIS'

Dressing
1 cup vegetable or walnut oil
¼ cup wine vinegar
½ teaspoon salt
⅛ teaspoon ground pepper
1 tablespoon chopped tarragon

Salad
4 heads bibb or Boston lettuce
1 tablespoon olive or vegetable oil
8 shrimp, peeled and deveined
   (see Glossary)
½ pound sea or bay scallops
2 shallots, finely minced
Salt and pepper to taste
1 tablespoon Pernod (see Glossary)
½ cup sliced mushrooms
1 red bell pepper, julienned (see
   Glossary)
16 cherry tomatoes, peeled

Garnish
2 hard boiled eggs, cut in quarters

To make dressing: Place all ingredients in pint jar and shake to combine well. Set aside.

To make salad: Separate lettuce into leaves and arrange 1 head on each of 4 salad plates. Set aside.

Heat oil in skillet over medium heat; add shrimp, scallops, and shallots. Season with salt and pepper and cook, stirring, for about 2 minutes or until almost done.

Warm pernod and add to skillet. Ignite to flambé. When flames die, add mushrooms and peppers, and saute for a moment. Add salad dressing and boil for 30 seconds. Add cherry tomatoes and heat gently to warm.

Arrange scallops, shrimp, and other hot ingredients attractively over the lettuce. Spoon dressing from the pan over the entire salad and garnish with egg quarters.

MAKES 4 SERVINGS

Masterson's Walnut Creek Station

850 S. Broadway, Walnut Creek, CA 94596;
(415) 934-1300.

Masterson's is many fascinating things. It's a restaurant whose offerings span the culinary spectrum from zesty breakfast, through mid-morning snacks, cocktail hour, dinner, and late-night hot fudge sundaes and pastries. It's also a meeting place, an entertainment spot, a place to have an old-timey photograph made, a place to hold a private party, and marvel at the in-house magician or chat with Farnsworth, Bat Masterson's favorite talking parrot, who has opinions on just about everything.

AVOCADO SEAFOOD SALAD

3 large lettuce leaves
2 cups shredded lettuce
1 avocado half, peeled
5 ounces cooked shrimp or
  crabmeat
1 hard boiled egg, sliced
1 lemon wedge
2 ripe olives
3 cherry tomatoes
1 sprig parsley
Salad dressing of your choice

Arrange lettuce leaves on 10-inch platter. Place shredded lettuce on lettuce leaves.

Slice avocado and place on lettuce. Mound shrimp/crab at left of avocado. Fan egg slices at right front. Place lemon wedge at left of shrimp/crab. Place olives between shrimp/crab and eggs. Arrange cherry tomatoes behind avocado.

Garnish with parsley sprig. Serve with choice of dressing.

MAKES 1 SERVING

Photograph, Page 9

Victor's

*The Westin St. Francis Hotel, Union Square,
335 Powell St., San Francisco, CA 94102;
(415) 956-7777.*

Victor's literally takes a legendary name to dramatic heights. Named in honor of Victor Hirtzler, the much-honored chef of the St. Francis from 1906 through 1925, Victor's is spectacularly situated on top of the 32-story hotel tower, with awe-inspiring views of the city and its world-famous bay. The menu honors Victor Hirtzler's memory, featuring many of his original recipes for dinner and Sunday brunch.

CHICKEN SALAD VICTOR

French Dressing
1/2 cup vegetable oil
2 tablespoons white wine vinegar
1/4 teaspoon black pepper
1/2 teaspoon salt

Chicken Salad
1 (3 1/2-pound) chicken
Water to cover
1 onion, halved
2 ribs celery, quartered
2 carrots, quartered
6 whole peppercorns
1/2 teaspoon thyme
1/2 cup cooked green beans, cut in
   bite-size pieces
1 cup cooked rice
4 tomatoes, peeled and quartered
1 truffle, sliced (optional)
1 teaspoon chopped parsley
1 teaspoon chopped chervil
3 fresh tarragon leaves, chopped
Lettuce leaves for serving

To make French dressing: Combine oil, vinegar, pepper, and salt in a covered jar. Shake to combine and set aside.

To prepare chicken salad: Boil chicken in water seasoned with onion, celery, carrots, peppercorns, and thyme about 40 minutes or until tender. Cool chicken in broth.

Remove chicken from broth; skin and dice meat into pieces of uniform size. Add green beans, rice, tomatoes, truffle, parsley, chervil, and tarragon.

Mix enough French dressing with chicken and vegetables to moisten. Serve on lettuce leaves.

Note: This is the original recipe of Chef Victor Hirtzler, chef of St. Francis, 1906-1925.

MAKES 6 TO 8 SERVINGS

3430 McHenry Ave., Modesto, CA 95350;
(209) 521-2920.

Whether you need to eat-and-run, or want to linger over your meal in comfort, Brawley's 24-hour family restaurants offer good value for your dining dollar. Relax in the cocktail lounge and enjoy sit-down dining there or in the main dining room. Try the unique flavor of Brawley's popular barbecue steak dinner with all the trimmings. Four locations to serve you: Modesto, Oakdale, Manteca, Sacramento; and another Brawley's coming soon in Sonora.

TACO SALAD WITH FLAIR

2 pounds ground beef
1/2 medium onion, chopped
1 package, Lawry's Taco
   Seasoning Mix
3/4 cup water
1 1/2 cups thousand island dressing
1/4 cup sour cream
Vegetable oil for frying
30 (10-inch) flour tortillas
Chopped lettuce for 6 servings
1 (16-ounce) can kidney beans
1/4 pound mild Cheddar cheese,
   grated
1/4 pound tortilla chips, broken
2 medium tomatoes, cut in 8
   wedges
18 whole pitted black olives
   (number per serving may vary)
6 tablespoons guacamole

Cook and stir ground beef and onions in skillet over medium heat until meat is brown and onion is tender. Drain fat and add taco seasoning and water. Simmer 15 to 20 minutes. Let cool.

Mix thousand island dressing with sour cream and set aside.

Heat oil in deep-fryer. Submerge tortilla in hot oil using a can or similar object placed even with one edge of tortilla. Remaining portion of tortilla will flute up forming a "basket." Fry until crispy and golden brown. Drain on paper towels.

Combine lettuce, seasoned meat, kidney beans, cheese, tortilla chips, and dressing. Mix well. It is important to combine only amounts that will be used immediately. Lettuce and tortilla chips will get soggy if mixed too soon before serving.

Serve mixture in tortilla basket on flat plates. Arrange 4 tomato wedges and 3 olives around top and spoon on 1 tablespoon guacamole for each serving.

Note: For variation use hot or mild salsa (see Glossary) in dressing or offer it on the side.

MAKES 6 SERVINGS

More than 350 locations all over California.

Californians-on-the-go know they can depend on the freshness and quality of the variety of foods served at the more than 350 Carl's Jr. Restaurants across the state. Among the most called-for items on the attractive menu are a variety of hamburgers, roast beef, steak, seafoods, chicken sandwiches, and desserts. The Serve-Yourself Salad Bars feature more than 20 different items. Guests can dine in carpeted dining rooms, or order from drive-through windows.

CARL'S JR. BLEU CHEESE SALAD DRESSING

1/2 cup mayonnaise
3/4 cup sour cream
1/4 cup bleu cheese
1/3 cup water
1 teaspoon vegetable oil
1 teaspoon chopped parsley
1/2 teaspoon salt
1/2 teaspoon garlic powder
1/4 teaspoon onion powder
1/4 teaspoon pepper

In medium bowl, combine mayonnaise, sour cream, blue cheese, water, and oil. Stir until well mixed.

Add parsley, salt, garlic powder, onion powder, and pepper and mix until thoroughly blended.

Store in refrigerator until ready to use with salad of your choice.

MAKES 1 PINT

Mr. Stox

1105 E. Katella Ave., Anaheim, CA 92805;
(714) 634-2994.

One of the Anaheim area's favorite dining places, Mr. Stox specializes in carefully prepared fresh seafoods, beef, veal, lamb, duckling, and chicken prepared in a variety of imaginative ways. These excellent dishes are complemented by a large selection of California and European wines. The Chateau Room, adjacent to the wine cellar, offers an intimate atmosphere for private gatherings of up to 30 guests. Mr. Stox is operated by Ron and Chick Marshall.

ONION TART (Tarte de Provence Aux Oignons)

Tomato Fondue
4 large ripe tomatoes
1 tablespoon butter
1/2 tablespoon garlic, finely
  chopped
1 tablespoon chopped fresh basil
Salt and pepper to taste

Tart Shells
1 cup all purpose flour
1/4 teaspoon salt
1/4 cup butter, chilled
3 tablespoons vegetable
  shortening, chilled
2 to 6 tablespoons ice water

To make tomato fondue: Core each tomato and cut a cross on the bottom of each about 1/8 inch deep. Place in a saucepan of boiling water for 1½ minutes. Quickly remove and peel outer skin from each tomato. Cut each peeled tomato in half across the middle and squeeze out seeds. Chop the tomatoes.

Melt the butter in heavy skillet and add the garlic. Cook slightly over medium high heat. Add tomatoes and basil and cook until tomatoes are very soft. Season with salt and pepper. Set aside.

To prepare tart shells: Sift flour and salt together into a bowl. Using pastry blender cut in butter and shortening until mixture is the size of small peas. Sprinkle water on, 1 tablespoon at a time, tossing mixture with pastry blender or a fork. When mixture holds together when pinched between thumb and forefinger, stop adding water.

Gather mixture into a ball and turn out onto floured surface. Divide in half, form into ball, and roll with a floured rolling pin to 1/8-inch thickness. Cut into 4 equal portions and line 4 (3-inch) tart shells, preferably with removable bottoms. Bake shells at 350 degrees F. for 8 to 10 minutes. Remove shells from oven and allow to cool on a rack.

ONION TART (Continued)
(Tarte de Provence Aux Oignons)

Tart Filling
3 medium sweet onions
4 leeks
2 tablespoons olive oil
1 tablespoon Herbs de Provence
   (see Note)
4 ounces California goat cheese

Garnish
4 sprigs fresh basil or mint

To prepare tart filling: Peel onions and remove core from the bottom. Slice across onions to create thin slices. Cut off the green section of the leeks leaving the last ½ inch attached to the white. Remove the root portion. Thoroughly wash to remove all sand. Split leeks in half end to end and slice each half on a bias.

Place olive oil in heavy skillet and heat over medium-high temperature. Add onions to hot oil and saute until transparent. Add leeks and cook 2 to 3 minutes. Onions should remain crisp and leeks will go limp. Add Herbs de Provence and cook 2 minutes. Remove from heat and allow to cool to room temperature.

Crumble goat cheese and divide equally among tart shells. Add onion mixture over cheese, over-filling the shells because the onions decrease in volume as they cook.

Bake the filled shells at 375 degrees F. for 12 to 15 minutes. They are ready when the shells turn a rich brown color. Reheat tomato fondue. Remove tarts from oven and quickly remove tarts from pans, onto 4 medium plates, each containing ¼ cup tomato fondue spread on the bottom. Garnish with a sprig of fresh basil or mint. Serve while still warm.

Note: Herbs de Provence is a mixture of basil, thyme, tarragon, rosemary, and sage. You may mix your own or purchase it from a gourmet shop.

MAKES 4 SERVINGS

*1740 S. Coast Hwy., Laguna Beach, CA 92651;
(714) 494-6588.*

At Tortilla Flats, Maria Aquiar's faithful followers view the breathtaking Catalina sunsets, while sipping fabulous margaritas and sampling some of Southern California's best Sonora-style Mexican cooking. Since 1959, Tortilla Flats has grown from a tiny "Laguna charm" house on Pacific Coast Highway, into today's magnificent Mexican colonial hacienda. To put you in the right mood for the Sunday Champagne Brunch, mariachi musicians are on hand for entertainment.

GREEN CORN TAMALES

*42 green chiles (California or
   Anaheim)
Vegetable oil for frying
5 pounds corn on cobs
1¹/₂ cups lard
1 cup plus 3 tablespoons butter
1 pound masa harina (corn flour
   available in Latin markets)
12 ounces Cheddar cheese, grated
12 ounces Monterrey Jack cheese,
   grated
¹/₂ cup sugar
¹/₃ cup salt
Pinch of baking powder
Hojas (corn husks)
Papel Para Tamales-papers (9-inch
   by 10-inch) or wax paper*

Deep-fry green chiles in hot oil until tender. To peel skin place hot chiles between two damp towels. When cool, skin will slip off. Slice lengthwise in ¹/₂-inch strips and set aside.

Remove corn from cobs and process corn in food processor or blender until finely pureed.

Beat lard and butter with electric mixer until fluffy.

Mix together corn, lard, butter, masa harina, cheeses, sugar, salt, and baking powder.

Place two corn husks together, overlaping half of each. Hold in palm of hand. Dip large mixing spoon into mixture and center about 8 tablespoons of mixture for each tamal on husks. Top with strips of green chile. Fold top and bottom of husk over mixture. Fold two other sides over to close tamal. Wrap each tamal diagonally in papel para tamal or wax paper.

Place on rack in large kettle, layering each row in between row below. Steam over hot water for 1¹/₂ hours or until cooked.

To serve, throw away papers. Peel back husks and fold under tamal. Garnish with remaining chile strips.

MAKES APPROXIMATELY 16 TAMALES

MEATS · PASTA

Miyako

139 S. Los Robles Ave., Pasadena, CA 91101;
(818) 795-7005.

In Japanese, Miyako means "capital city." In Pasadena, Orange, and Torrance, Miyako stands for fine Japanese restaurants that specialize in authentic sukiyaki dining. The original Miyako opened in 1959 in the Livingstone Hotel in Pasadena. The serene atmosphere, highlighted by waterfalls and Japanese gardens, made it an immediate favorite, and led to the establishment of new Miyakos in Orange and Torrance.

SUKIYAKI

Sukiyaki Cooking Sauce
2 ounces sake (Japanese rice wine)
1/2 cup Japanese soy sauce
1/4 cup sugar
*1/2 cup consomme or beef stock
  (see Basic Stocks)*

Sukiyaki
*1 1/2 pounds top sirloin, thinly
  sliced*
1 1/2 pounds onions, sliced
*8 (1-inch) cubes tofu (see
  Glossary)*
*2 bunches green onions, cut in
  2-inch lengths*
*1 cup shirataki noodles (available in
  Oriental markets)*
4 large mushrooms, cut in half
1/2 pound fresh bean sprouts
1/2 can bamboo shoots, sliced
4 cups cooked rice

To make sukiyaki cooking sauce: Heat sake, soy sauce, sugar, and stock in small saucepan until sugar dissolves.

To prepare sukiyaki: Arrange meat and vegetables in groups on a large platter, placed near electric skillet. Preheat skillet to 350 degrees F. Add vegetables, keeping them in separate groups. Add meat and cooking sauce. Cook 3 to 5 minutes so that vegetables remain crisp. Turn vegetables and meat over once during cooking. Serve with hot rice while vegetables are still crisp. Sugar and more sauce may be added if desired.

MAKES 4 SERVINGS

The Sycamore Inn

*8318 Foothill Blvd., Cucamonga, CA 91730;
(714) 982-1104.*

The Sycamore Inn carries on a hospitable tradition that goes back to the late 1840s, when a little trailside inn served home-cooked meals to passengers on the Butterfield Stagecoach Line. Standing in the shade of a sycamore grove, today's Inn takes great pride in its excellent food, wines, and genuine hospitality. The Inn's solid culinary reputation is the responsibility of Chef Parrella, who has been preparing award-winning Italian, American, and California dishes here since 1949.

FILET OF BEEF PROVENCALE

Provencale Sauce

1 pound carrots, sliced ⅛ inch
   thick
2 medium onions, coarsely
   chopped
2 tablespoons vegetable oil
2 bay leaves
¼ teaspoon basil
½ teaspoon oregano
¼ teaspoon salt
¼ teaspoon pepper
4 ounces sherry
1½ pounds tomatoes, peeled
   and chopped
1 (12-ounce) can mushrooms,
   with liquid
½ cup sliced black olives
1¼ cups white sauce (see Basic
   Sauces)

4 (6-ounce) tenderloin filets
8 slices bread, trimmed and
   toasted

To make provencale sauce: Saute carrots and onions in 1 tablespoon oil in skillet, over medium heat, until soft but not brown.

Add bay leaves, basil, oregano, salt, pepper, and sherry. Cook until carrots are tender but not soft. Add tomatoes, mushrooms with liquid, and olives. Cook until all vegetables are done. Add white sauce and stir well.

Cut filets into 2 horizontal slices and saute to desired doneness in another skillet with remaining vegetable oil. Add to skillet with provencale sauce and heat. Serve filet slices on toast with sauce.

MAKES 4 SERVINGS

Griswold's Indian Hill

555 W. Foothill Blvd., Claremont, CA 91711; (714) 626-2411.

The Indian Hill Restaurant at Griswold's Inn has been given the magic touch of success by longtime California restaurateurs A.L. and Betty Sanford. A favorite Claremont dining place since 1968, the restaurant has been honored with the California Restaurant Writers' Award for the past dozen years, and received the Gourmet Diners Club of America's Silver Spoon Award in 1982. The 282-room Inn has a charming Early California decor.

EMINCE DE BOEUF STROGANOFF

Sauce
1 medium onion, chopped
1/2 pound mushrooms, sliced
3 tablespoons butter
Salt to taste
2 teaspoons chopped shallots
8 ounces sherry
1 teaspoon glace de viande
   (see Glossary)
1 quart sour cream
1 to 2 teaspoons paprika
Monosodium glutamate
White pepper to taste
1 tablespoon cornstarch dissolved
   in 1/4 cup sherry
1/2 cup heavy cream, or more
   if needed

Meat
2 pounds trimmed beef tenderloin
Salt and pepper to taste
2 tablespoons butter
2 tablespoons vegetable oil
2 shallots, chopped
2 ounces sherry

Garnish
2 tablespoons chopped chives

To make sauce: Saute onions and mushrooms in butter over low heat for 5 minutes. Add salt and cook, covered, for 3 more minutes. After mushrooms are brown, stir in shallots. Add sherry, glace de viande, and sour cream. Mix in thoroughly. Add paprika and mix well. Add a little monosodium glutamate, pepper, and taste for salt.

Heat sauce and stir in cornstarch mixture, a little at a time. Sauce should be on the thick side.

Add the cream to taste. If sauce is too thick, add more cream. Taste for seasoning. Set aside sauce in saucepan. Sauce may be prepared ahead of time and reheated before serving.

To prepare meat: Slice tenderloin into fingers about 1/4 inch thick and 1 1/2 inches long. Salt and pepper meat.

Heat butter and oil over high heat in skillet. Add beef in batches, cooking 1 to 2 minutes per side. Do not add too much meat at a time, or the meat will boil and not saute. Remove to a colander to drain off grease.

Return meat to skillet, and add shallots and sherry. Cook until sherry is reduced by one-third. Strain the liquid into the prepared sauce and mix it in well. Reheat sauce, add to meat, and bring to a boil. Sprinkle with chives and serve.

Serve with rice pilaf, wild rice, or boiled potatoes.

MAKES 6 SERVINGS

Angie's

11700 Wilshire Blvd., Los Angeles, CA 90025;
(213) 477-1517.

From a bountiful hamburger to delectable veal and pasta dishes, and crepes with an exotic Mediteranean flavor, Angie's has the answer to most of the appetite needs of its discriminating Brentwood patrons. Operated by Angelo and Ann Pappas and their sons Louis and Gregg, Angie's also offers a choice of dining atmosphere, from casual to three formal rooms. One of the most called-for dishes is "Angie's Favorite", a blend of chicken, veal, Greek sausage, mushrooms, peppers, and onions.

MOUSSAKA

Eggplant
4 eggplants
Salt

Filling
2 large onions, chopped
1/4 cup vegetable oil
4 pounds ground beef
1 tablespoon salt
1 tablespoon cinnamon
1 tablespoon pepper
Pinch sugar
1 (6-ounce) can tomato paste,
    mixed with 1 quart water
1 bunch parsley, chopped
1 cup grated Cheddar cheese
2 eggs, beaten lightly

Béchamel Sauce
1 cup butter
1 cup flour
1 quart milk, scalded
Salt to taste
1 tablespoon white pepper
1 tablespoon nutmeg
1/2 cup grated Cheddar cheese
4 eggs, lightly beaten

Olive oil for frying

To prepare eggplant: Slice eggplants into 3/4-inch slices. Salt both sides and allow to set 15 minutes. Press out excess water.

To make filling: In skillet over moderate heat saute onions in oil until transparent. Add meat, salt, cinnamon, pepper, and sugar and saute until brown. Add tomato paste and simmer for 20 minutes. Remove from heat, mix in parsley, cheese, and beaten eggs.

To make béchamel sauce: Melt butter in saucepan, add flour, stirring to make a roux (see Glossary). Add milk stirring constantly with wire whisk. Add salt, pepper, nutmeg, and cheese. Cook on low heat for 10 to 15 minutes, remove from heat, and stir in beaten eggs. Return to heat 5 more minutes to finish cooking.

Cover bottom of skillet with a thin coat of olive oil and brown eggplant lightly. Place half of eggplant slices in bottom of a large ovenproof casserole. Sprinkle with grated cheese and pour half of meat mixture on top. Place another layer of eggplant on top and cover with remainder of meat mixture. Cover with béchamel sauce and bake at 375 degrees F. until brown on top, approximately 1 hour.

MAKES 8 TO 10 SERVINGS

El Torito

24301 Avenida de Carlota, Laguna Hills, CA 92653; (714) 951-9137.

America was largely the land of hamburgers and hot dogs when Larry J. Cano brought his family's recipes from Sonora, Mexico back in 1954, and introduced them at the first El Torito Restaurant in Encino, California. Word quickly spread about El Torito's tasty chimichangas — a huge flour tortilla stuffed with mildly seasoned beef, pork, and Mexican-style vegetables — as well as their burritos, chile rellenos, tacos, and other specialties. Today El Torito is one of America's largest Mexican restaurant organizations with over 35 locations in southern California, and in 20 states nationwide.

EL TORITO CHIMICHANGA

2 tablespoons lard
2 pounds pork tenderloin, diced
  into $1/2$-inch cubes
1 pound onions, diced
1 tablespoon salt
1 tablespoon garlic powder
$1^1/4$ teaspoons black pepper
1 teaspoon ground cumin
1 small bay leaf
$3/4$ teaspoon oregano
$2/3$ cup canned crushed tomatoes
$2/3$ cup tomato sauce
1 to 2 Serrano chiles
Lard for frying
1 pound Anaheim chiles, seeded
  and diced
$1/4$ cup cilantro leaves
  (see Glossary)
$3/4$ cup water
$1/4$ pound tomatoes, sliced
1 tablespoon chicken stock (see
  Basic Stocks)
1 teaspoon monosodium
  glutamate
1 tablespoon Worcestershire sauce
$1/2$ cup flour
8 (13-inch) flour tortillas

Heat 2 tablespoons lard in Dutch oven or electric skillet set at 325 degrees F. Add pork and brown slowly over moderate heat.

Add onions, cover, and continue to cook over moderate heat until meat is tender, about 45 minutes. Watch to see that juices do not cook away. If necessary, add a small quantity of water to keep meat from sticking.

In bowl, combine salt, garlic powder, pepper, cumin, bay leaf, and oregano. Add seasonings to meat along with crushed tomatoes and tomato sauce and cook 5 minutes longer.

Heat 1 to $1^1/2$ inches lard in deep skillet. Place Serrano chiles in hot lard for a few minutes to blister and then combine with cilantro and water in blender and blend until pureed. Add to meat mixture along with Anaheim chiles, sliced tomatoes, chicken stock, monosodium glutamate, Worcestershire, and flour. Cook, stirring until blended.

To make chimichangas, heat flour tortillas, covered, in a warm oven until pliable. Place $1/2$ cup meat mixture in center of each flour tortilla. Fold in sides, then roll. Place chimichanga seam side down in hot lard. Press down with spatula until tortilla is crisp and lightly browned. Turn to brown both sides. Drain on paper towels.

MAKES 8 CHIMICHANGAS

El Cholo

1121 S. Western Ave., Los Angeles, CA 90006;
(213) 734-2773.

Originally located in a small bungalow on the Los Angeles outskirts, this 56-year-old partriarch of the El Cholo Restaurant family is now part of Los Angeles' bustling inner city. The humble bungalow has grown into a beautiful restaurant serving such traditional Mexican favorites as green corn tamales, giant-sized burritos, vegetable tostados, and puffy chile rellenos. El Cholo's award-winning margaritas are blended from Cointreau and premium Jose Cuervo "1800" tequila.

EL CHOLO TOSTADA COMPUESTA

4 crisp fried tortillas
1 cup refried beans
¼ cup chopped chorizo (Mexican spiced sausage available in Latin markets)
1 cup shredded Cheddar cheese
1 head lettuce, shredded
1 cup sliced red cabbage
1 cup diced jicama (a vegetable available in Latin markets)
1 cup fresh cooked peas
1 cup fresh cooked green beans
1 cup diced beets
1 cup diced or shredded carrots
1 cup taco sauce
1 cup shredded Monterrey Jack cheese
1 cup French dressing of your choice

Garnish (optional)
Sliced tomatoes
Avocado
Watercress
Cilantro
  (see Glossary)

Place tortillas on plate. Cover each with one-fourth of the beans. Top with chorizo and Cheddar cheese, again dividing into fourths.

Place tortillas in broiler or oven to melt cheese.

Remove from oven and arrange lettuce on top and then all remaining vegetables.

Top with taco sauce, sprinkle with Monterrey Jack cheese and French dressing.

Garnish with sliced tomatoes and avocado, pieces of watercress or cilantro, if desired.

MAKES 4 SERVINGS

Photograph, Page 9

At Marty's

8657 West Pico Blvd., Los Angeles, CA 90035;
(213) 272-1048.

Delightful...delicious...delectable...delovely! Enter at Marty's and you enter the enchanting Art Deco world of Manhattan's East Side circa the 1930s and '40s. In this mesmerizing time-capsule of mirrored and sculpted glass, whimsical fixtures, and statuary you would hardly be surprised to find Bogie and Bergman sequestered in a hidden-away corner. The cosmopolitan cuisine — seafoods, veal, chicken, salads, pastas, and vegetarian dishes — matches the sophisticated surroundings.

LAMBUCCO

Butter-mint Paste
1 cup butter, softened
1/2 bunch fresh mint, chopped
6 to 12 cloves fresh garlic,
    chopped
1/4 pound bacon, chopped
1/2 bunch freshly chopped parsley
1/4 cup red wine vinegar

Tomato Sauce
1 (16-ounce) can whole tomatoes,
    crushed, with juice
2 cups tomato juice
1 teaspoon tomato paste
6 bay leaves, crushed
1 teaspoon dill
1 teaspoon rosemary
1 teaspoon whole thyme
1/2 teaspoon ground pepper
1 tablespoon Worcestershire sauce
2 (10-ounce) cans chicken broth
1 (10-ounce) can beef broth

Lamb
4 to 6 fresh lamb shanks, trimmed
    of gristle and membrane
3 onions, sliced in circles
6 carrots, sliced in wedges
1 pound pitted prunes

To prepare butter-mint paste: Combine butter, mint, garlic, bacon, parsley, and vinegar and mix well. Set aside. Makes about 1 1/4 cup butter-mint paste.

To prepare tomato sauce: Combine crushed tomatoes, tomato juice, tomato paste, bay leaves, dill, rosemary, thyme, pepper, Worcestershire sauce, chicken broth, beef broth, and one-fourth of the butter-mint paste in a saucepan. Simmer 30 minutes and set aside.

To prepare lamb: Meanwhile brown lamb shanks in ovenproof pan on top of stove at high heat in one-fourth of the butter-mint paste, turning constantly until dark brown.

Drain pan. Arrange shanks in the pan and cover them with onion circles and carrot wedges. Ladle one-half of the tomato sauce over lamb, carrots, and onions. Cover with foil and place in oven.

Bake at 350 degrees F. for 1 hour. Remove pan from oven, remove foil, dot with remaining butter-mint paste, and return pan to oven, uncovered, and cook 1 hour more, basting at 30 minutes.

Remove from oven, rotate the shanks to the top, and carrots and onions to the bottom of pan. Add prunes and return to oven for additional 30 minutes or until meat is tender.

MAKES 4 TO 6 SERVINGS

The Vineyard

The Century Plaza Hotel, 2025 Avenue of the Stars, Los Angeles, CA 90067; (213) 277-2000.

At the Vineyard, one in the galaxy of fine dining places in the Century Plaza, the emphasis is on wine, California and continental cuisines. The innovative menu artfully combines seasonal California foods with such haute cuisine mainstays as truffles and caviar. Menus change with the seasons. A game menu in March features Scottish venison and grouse; a summer special brings forth salads and California lamb in mustard sauce.

RACK OF LAMB WITH DRIED FIGS "CALIFORNIA STYLE"

Rack of Lamb
Vegetable oil for browning
1 rack of lamb
2 tablespoons butter, melted
1 clove garlic, minced
Salt and pepper to taste
1/2 teaspoon powdered English mustard
2 tablespoons honey
1/4 teaspoon powdered ginger
1 tablespoon white wine

Fig Topping
2 teaspoons butter
1/2 medium onion, chopped
1 clove garlic, minced
1 cup chopped dried California figs
1/2 cup chopped mango chutney
3 tablespoons white wine
1/2 teaspoon powdered English mustard
1/2 teaspoon ground coriander
1 teaspoon powdered ginger
Pinch of nutmeg
1 cup crushed peanuts
1 cup fresh white bread crumbs
1/2 cup chopped parsley
1/2 cup chopped chives

To prepare rack of lamb: In heavy skillet heat enough oil to cover bottom of pan. Brown rack of lamb on both sides over high heat. Combine butter and garlic and brush on lamb. Salt and pepper to taste. Roast at 375 degrees F. to an internal temperature of 140 degrees F. for medium rare or to desired degree of doneness.

To prepare fig topping: Place butter in pan, melt, and saute onions and garlic. Add figs, chutney, wine, mustard, coriander, ginger, and nutmeg. Mix with peanuts, bread crumbs, parsley, and chives.

Press mixture onto top of rack of lamb and return lamb to oven for 5 minutes to brown. Slice between ribs to serve.

MAKES 2 SERVINGS

1500 S. Raymond Ave., Fullerton, CA 92631;
(714) 635-9000.

The legend of Ruby Begonia has its roots in the traditions of the Deep South. Ruby's father, so it is told, was a wealthy plantation owner who honored his vivacious daughter by naming a bright red, ever-blooming begonia after her. Ruby Begonia's Restaurant recreates the charm of this bygone era with intimate dining, fireside seating, greenery, and an extensive menu that includes numerous American/continental favorites. Ruby's is renowned for its elaborate Sunday Champagne Brunch.

VEAL SCALLOPINI MARSALA

2 pounds filet of veal, cut in
   12 thin slices
Flour for dredging
1/2 cup butter or olive oil
1 clove garlic, crushed
14 ounces fresh mushrooms, sliced
4 shallots, finely diced (Optional)
2 ounces Marsala wine (or dry
   white wine)
Salt and pepper to taste

Garnish
Lemon wedges

Pound veal slices with a mallet to flatten. Dredge veal in flour.

Heat butter or olive oil in large frying pan to moderate temperature and saute slices, quickly, until golden brown. Add crushed garlic, mushrooms, shallots, and wine.

Cover and simmer 6 to 8 minutes. Season with salt and pepper. Serve with lemon wedges.

MAKES 6 SERVINGS

The Sardine Factory

701 Wave St., Monterey, CA 93940;
(408) 373-3775.

On colorful Cannery Row in Monterey, The Sardine Factory is acclaimed for its excellent cuisine, superb wine list, and flawless service. Diners usually begin their adventure in the cocktail lounge, whose walls chronicle the Row's long, rich history. From there, the choice of dining venues includes the Victorian-style Captain's Room, the glass-domed Conservatory, and the intimate Wine Cellar, whose racks and rock walls give the snug feeling of a cavern.

VEAL CARDINAL

6 (6-ounce) Australian lobster tails
1¼ pounds veal, cut in thin slices
  (we prefer Wisconsin white
  veal from short loin)
Flour for dredging
2 tablespoons butter
1½ pounds fresh mushrooms,
  sliced
½ cup dry sauterne wine
2 tablespoons chopped parsley
2 tablespoons chopped garlic
Juice of 1 lemon
Salt and pepper to taste

Dredge lobster and veal in flour. Heat butter in skillet and saute lobster lightly. Add mushrooms and continue cooking until mushrooms are tender. Remove lobster and mushrooms with a slotted spoon and set aside.

In same skillet saute veal until golden brown on both sides, adding more butter if necessary. Return lobster and mushrooms to skillet.

Add sauterne and ignite to flambé. When flames have subsided, add parsley, garlic, and lemon juice. Simmer for 2 to 3 minutes, add salt and pepper, and serve.

MAKES 6 SERVINGS

Photograph, Page 10

120 Marina Dr., Rio Vista, CA 94571;
(707) 374-2315.

At The Point Restaurant in northern California's Delta Marina yacht harbor, guests enjoy great California seafood, beef, and continental specialties, like the house's delicious veal piccata. The charming setting overlooks the Sacramento River. The dining room, cocktail lounge, and banquet and meeting rooms are only a few steps from the restaurant's 400-foot guest dock.

VEAL PICCATA

12 thin slices of veal (2 pounds)
Salt and pepper to taste
1 cup flour
1/4 cup grated Parmesan cheese
1/2 cup olive oil
1/2 medium onion, diced
1 clove garlic, minced
1/2 pound mushrooms, sliced
1/2 cup sherry
1 cup veal or chicken stock (see
   Basic Stocks)
Juice of 1 lemon
1/2 cup capers
2 tablespoons chopped parsley

Pound veal slices with mallet to flatten. Season with salt and pepper and dredge in flour mixed with Parmesan cheese.

Heat oil in large skillet and add as many pieces of veal as the skillet will hold in one layer. Cook over high heat to brown on both sides, approximately 1 minute on each side.

Transfer veal to platter and keep warm. Repeat until all veal is browned.

Combine onion, garlic, and mushrooms in skillet and saute 3 to 4 minutes. Add sherry, stock, lemon juice, capers, and parsley. Lower heat and return veal pieces to skillet, stirring slowly to cook evenly until the sauce coats all pieces.

Serve with rice.

MAKES 6 SERVINGS

Alfredo's

Westin South Coast Plaza Hotel, 666 Anton Blvd.,
Orange County, CA 92626;
(714) 540-2500.

Elegant Northern Italian cuisine...a superb selection of wines and champagnes...a lovely dining room filled with the romantic sounds of a harp. All these elements enhance luncheon, dinner, and Sunday brunch at Alfredo's in the luxurious Westin South Coast Plaza Hotel. Along with its sumptuous, award-winning Northern Italian dishes, Alfredo's menu is highlighted by fresh seafoods, beef, chicken, duck, lamb, and lavish desserts prepared under the direction of the restaurant's French-trained executive chef.

VEAL VENNINI

Basil Hollandaise
2 tablespoons butter
4 tablespoons chopped fresh basil
1 cup Hollandaise sauce (see Basic
    Sauces)

Veal
6 scaloppine of veal
Flour for dredging
5 tablespoons butter
1 teaspoon chopped shallots
$1/2$ cup Marsala wine
Salt and pepper to taste
$1/2$ cup veal stock (see Basic Stocks)
4 medallions cooked lobster tail

To make basil Hollandaise: Melt butter in saucepan and saute basil for 3 minutes over medium heat, stirring occasionally. Remove from heat and whisk Hollandaise sauce into basil mixture. Set aside in pan.

To prepare veal: Saute veal in 2 tablespoons of butter. Set aside and keep veal warm in very low oven.

Add shallots and wine to pan and reduce by half. Add veal stock and again reduce by half.

Remove pan from heat, whisk in remaining butter, and salt and pepper to taste.

Place half of warmed basil Hollandaise on 2 serving plates. Place veal scaloppine on top of sauce. Arrange lobster medallions on top of veal. Spread lobster with remaining half of basil Hollandaise sauce.

MAKES 2 SERVINGS

Photograph, Page 9

Francois'

Arco Plaza, 555 S. Flower St., Los Angeles, CA 90071;
(213) 680-2727.

At Francois', the first hint of the elegance to come is your entry into a stone-lined hallway illuminated by chandeliers, and banked on one side by iron-gated alcoves that hold the restaurant's fabulous selection of California and European wines. Your luncheon and dinner will require a delicious choice of such dishes as roast duckling flambé au calvados, boeuf Wellington, and salmon cooked in a paper shell with vegetables and wine butter sauce. Service, of course, is impeccable.

MEDALLION DE VEAU CALIFORNIA

Sauce Velouté
3 tablespoons butter
1/4 onion, sliced
4 tablespoons flour
1 cup milk
Salt and pepper to taste
Nutmeg to taste
1 egg yolk
1/4 cup heavy cream, whipped

Veal
Salt and pepper to taste
8 (2 1/2-ounce) pieces of veal
     tenderloin
3 tablespoons flour
4 tablespoons butter
1/4 cup dry white wine
2 avocados, peeled and sliced
8 (1-ounce) slices goose liver pâté
Paprika

To make sauce velouté: Melt butter in pan and saute onion. Do not brown. Add flour and mix. Do not allow to change color. Add milk, a little at a time, stirring constantly. Bring to a boil and continue stirring. Add salt, pepper, and nutmeg to taste. Continue cooking sauce, stirring occasionally, for about 15 to 20 minutes.

To finish sauce, strain and allow to cool slightly. Add egg yolk, beating well. Gently fold in whipped cream. while sauce is cooking, prepare veal.

To prepare veal: Salt and pepper veal. Dust with flour. Melt butter in frying pan and saute veal for 6 to 7 minutes, turning occasionally, until nicely browned. Drain pan and return veal to stove. Add wine and cook to reduce by half.

Place veal on plate with avocado and goose liver on top. Pour sauce velouté over and sprinkle with paprika. Place under broiler until lightly browned.

Note: For an optional method of serving, add 4 tablespoons brown sauce (see Basic Sauces) to the frying pan with the wine and mix well. Remove pan from stove and add butter. Pour this sauce onto serving plate and place veal on top of sauce. Finish recipe as above.

MAKES 4 SERVINGS

305 N. Harbor Blvd., Fullerton, CA 92632;
(714) 525-5682.

Opened in 1970 as a restaurant serving traditional French cooking, The Cellar has ambitiously expanded its menu to include other adventuresome and creative cuisines. Proprietor Louis Schnelli and chef Salvatore Troia regularly visit Europe, seeking new ideas and exciting new dishes. The restaurant is about four miles from Disneyland, in the vaulted brick cellar of an old hotel known as the Villa Del Sol. The warm, cozy dining rooms are conducive to the enjoyment of great food and wines.

MOUSSELINE DE VEAU AU RIESLING (Veal Mousseline with Riesling Wine Sauce)

Riesling Wine Sauce
1 cup heavy cream
1 1/2 cups Riesling wine
1/3 cup demi-glace (see Glossary)
Salt and pepper to taste
1 cup Hollandaise sauce (see
  Basic Sauces)

Veal Mousseline
2 1/4 pounds veal, trimmed of
  fat and skin
1/4 teaspoon ground nutmeg
1/2 teaspoon powdered English
  mustard
1 cup cold egg whites, lightly
  beaten
3 cups cold heavy cream,
  lightly beaten
Sea salt and ground white pepper
  to taste
1 bay leaf
1 sprig thyme

Garnish
2 avocados, peeled and cut in
  slices
24 to 36 seedless grapes

To make Riesling wine sauce: In heavy saucepan boil cream until it is reduced by half. In another saucepan reduce wine by half. Combine the two liquids with the demi-glace and reduce until there is 1 cup of liquid. Set aside sauce. Make Hollandaise sauce and set aside. Just before serving stir the Hollandaise into the reduced sauce.

To make veal mousseline: Cut veal in 1 1/2-inch to 2-inch strips. Sprinkle with nutmeg and English mustard. Put in food processor equipped with steel blade and process until paste-like consistency. Do not overprocess. Pass this through a wire sieve using a plastic spatula, place in bowl, cover, and chill in refrigerator for 2 hours.

Remove from refrigerator, place bowl in larger bowl of ice and add egg whites in small amounts until all is incorporated. Add cream in small amounts until all is incorporated. Add salt and pepper to taste, keeping in mind that the finished product will taste less strong than the uncooked mixture.

Butter a 2-quart enameled cast iron terrine (pâté) mold and fill with mixture. Put two halves of bay leaf and a small sprig of thyme on top and cover with lid. Bake on middle oven shelf at 350 degrees F. for 35 minutes.

To serve cut the still-warm and unmolded mousseline into 12 or 16 slices. Serve two per person, and place on hot dinner plates. Garnish each slice with avocado slices and 4 grapes. Cover the slices with the Riesling sauce. Place the plates under the broiler until mousseline is lightly colored and serve immediately.

Note: Veal mousseline may be prepared ahead and reheated in the oven.

MAKES 6 TO 8 SERVINGS

The Carnelian Room

Bank of America World Headquarters Bldg.,
555 California St., San Francisco, CA 94104;
(415) 433-7500.

An elevator whisks you to this mesmerizing room in only 32 seconds. Here, 52 stories high, 779 feet above the world, The Carnelian Room offers you San Francisco, spread in a 360-degree panorama. The dining is exquisite, the service impeccable. A team of international chefs prepares a rainbow of American and continental dishes, served in dining rooms that seat as many as 200, or as few as just you and your companion.

LES MEDAILLONS DE CHEVREUIL AUX CHANTERELLES
(Medallions of Venison with Chanterelles)

Venison Marinade
1 quart port wine
1 cup red wine vinegar
2 bay leaves
1/2 cup pickling spice
1/4 cup sugar
Salt and pepper to taste

Venison
1 (7-pound) loin of venison

Venison Sauce
1 cup cooking oil
1 cup coarsely chopped celery
1 cup coarsely chopped onions
1 cup coarsely chopped carrots
2 tablespoons tomato paste
1 cup flour
2 quarts chicken stock (see Basic
    Stocks)
3 tablespoons currant jelly
1 cup Madeira
Salt and pepper to taste

To make venison marinade: Combine all ingredients for marinade and set aside.

To prepare venison: Bone venison, reserving bones. Trim the loin well and cut into 16 (3-ounce) medallions. Pound the medallions to flatten and marinate, covered, in refrigerator for 72 hours. Reserve 1 cup marinade for venison sauce.

To prepare venison sauce: Chop venison bones into small pieces. Brown bones in oil in roasting pan over medium heat. Add chopped celery, onions, and carrots and cook until brown, stirring occasionally. Add tomato paste and flour and brown for 2 minutes. Add stock and let simmer for 1 hour.

Then add 1 cup venison marinade, currant jelly, Madeira, and season with salt and pepper. Let simmer for 15 minutes and strain sauce.

To make garnish: Peel, halve, and core apples. Blanche apples in 1 quart of boiling water, with sugar, lemon juice, and white wine. Be sure the apples stay al dente (see Glossary) or crisp. Allow apples to cool and place in a buttered baking dish. Fill apple halves with sugar-glazed marrons. Sprinkle apples with sugar. Add dash of white wine. Bake at 425 degrees F. for 5 to 8 minutes.

LES MEDAILLONS DE CHEVREUIL AUX CHANTERELLES (Continued)
(Medallions of Venison with Chanterelles)

Garnish
8 medium apples
1 quart water
1 cup sugar
1 cup lemon juice
1 cup white wine
Butter
16 canned, sugar-glazed marrons
  (chestnuts, available in
  gourmet shops)
Sugar for sprinkling
Dash of white wine

Chanterelles Sauce
1 (16-ounce) tin chanterelles (see
  Glossary)
6 tablespoons finely chopped
  shallots
2 tablespoons butter
¼ cup brandy
¼ cup Madeira
1 cup heavy cream

Flour for dredging
Vegetable oil for frying

To make chanterelles sauce: Drain juice from chanterelles. Reconstitute with water if using dried chanterelles, then drain. Saute shallots in butter until golden . Add chanterelles, flame with brandy and Madeira. Add 3 cups venison sauce and the heavy cream. Simmer 10 minutes.

Remove venison from marinade and dry the medallions. Dust lightly with flour. Place medallions in hot oil in skillet and saute to desired degree of doneness.

Arrange on platter, place apples filled with marrons around the venison. Top medallions with chanterelles sauce. Serve with wild rice or potato croquettes accompanied with lingonberries.

MAKES 8 SERVINGS

The Jolly Roger

203 Marine Ave., Balboa Island, CA 92662;
(714) 673-8720.

The Jolly Roger has been a landmark synonymous with Balboa Island since Art Salisbury first opened the doors back in 1948. During those past 35 years, the original small coffee shop has added a fountain, patio area, and a comfortable dining room displaying an abundance of nautical artifacts. But the "J.R.'s" original hospitality and feeling of welcome has been maintained, on Balboa Island and in more than 50 other Jolly Roger Restaurants in California and Hawaii.

SUZIE Q

1 knockwurst (or weiner)
1 bacon slice
1 French roll
2 tablespoons shredded Cheddar
  cheese
2 tablespoons barbecue sauce

Wrap knockwurst with 1 slice uncooked bacon and fasten with toothpick. Place on hot grill and cook until bacon is brown, turning for evenness. Remove toothpick and place in French roll.

Sprinkle with grated cheese, place in grill, and cover grill to melt cheese.

Serve with barbecue sauce.

MAKES 1 SERVING

1135 Morro St., San Luis Obispo, CA 93406;
(805) 543-9268.
611 Grand Ave., Arroyo Grande, CA.

If variety is truly the spice of life, then it is found in abundance at Farley's. On any given day, guests may experience Mandarin duck from China, chicken paprikash from Hungary, and any number of American and international surprises. The origianl Farley's was opened in historic San Luis Obispo more than 25 years ago. The spice of life came to Arroyo Grande, further down the central coast, in 1979.

BAKED COUNTRY RABBIT CHASSUERS

2 rabbits, cut in 4-ounce to 5-ounce
   portions
Flour for dredging
Salt and pepper to taste
Garlic powder to taste
Monosodium glutamate
1 cup vegetable oil
1 bunch green onions, julienned
   (see Glossary)
1 pound medium whole
   mushrooms
2 (16-ounce) cans tomatoes
1 (16-ounce) can sliced apples
2 cups apple juice
3 tablespoons seasoned chicken
   stock base
2 tablespoons sugar
1/3 teaspoon thyme
1/2 cup sauterne wine
2 cups water

Dredge rabbit in a mixture of flour, salt, pepper, garlic powder,and monosodium glutamate. Cook rabbit in oil, covered, in a Dutch oven at 350 degrees F. for about 45 minutes.

Add remaining ingredients, lower heat, and cook at 250 degrees F. for 1½ hours, stirring gently about every 15 minutes.

Note: If the rabbits are not fairly young, parboil for 2 hours before starting the flouring procedure. This will insure tenderness.

MAKES 8 SERVINGS

Photograph, Page 11

The Cliff House

1090 Point Lobos, at Seal Rocks, San Francisco, CA 94121; (415) 387-5847.

Upstairs is one of two fine restaurants at the world-famous Cliff House on San Francisco's Seal Rocks. Upstairs is the city's omelette capital, offering a tempting choice of more than 45 variations on this popular culinary theme. Also during the day, Upstairs will tempt your palate with homemade soups, salads, and gourmet sandwiches. During the evening hours, the menu is augmented by pasta, seafood, chicken, quiche, and ribs. There is always a sensational seacoast view.

FETTUCCINI AL PESTO

1 cup firmly packed chopped parsley
1/2 cup olive oil
1/2 cup cream
1/2 cup butter, softened
3 or 4 cloves garlic, crushed
1 teaspoon or more salt
1/2 teaspoon freshly ground pepper
1 cup grated Parmesan cheese
1 cup chopped fresh basil leaves, firmly packed
1/2 cup chopped walnuts
2 tablespoons boiling water
2 pounds fettuccini
8 quarts boiling salted water

Place parsley, olive oil, cream, butter, garlic, 1 tablespoon salt, pepper, cheese, basil, and walnuts in a saucepan and stir. Reduce heat to low, add 2 tablespoons water and cover. Simmer over medium heat for 10 minutes, stirring frequently.

Meanwhile, cook fettuccini in 8 quarts boiling salted water according to package directions. Drain and toss the sauce lightly with the fettuccini and serve immediately.

MAKES 8 SERVINGS

The Rogue

*Wharf No. 2, Monterey, CA 93940;
(408) 372-4586.*

From the windows of The Rogue, diners drink in the dramatic panoramas of Monterey Bay, the hills, the marina, sailboats, fishing boats, seabirds diving for their dinner, and frisky otters at play. Located on Monterey's Marina, surrounded by early California history and the romance of the sea, diners also enjoy great cocktails and wines, seafoods from local waters and far-off seas, and the choicest steaks, veal, and lamb. Owners Ted Balestreri and Bert Cutino have created a truly unique dining experience.

LINGUINI PESCADORI

8 sea scallops
8 large prawns, peeled
2 tablespoons olive oil
*2 tomatoes, peeled, seeded, and
   crushed*
1 tablespoon chopped fresh basil
1 tablespoon finely chopped garlic
4 sprigs parsley, chopped
8 clams in shells
1/4 cup water
Salt to taste
*1 pound thin noodles, cooked
   al dente (see Glossary)*
2 tablespoons unsalted butter
2 tablespoons heavy cream
*1 tablespoon grated Parmesan
   cheese*

In skillet saute scallops and prawns in 1 tablespoon of olive oil.

In another skillet place remaining tablespoon of oil and add tomatoes, basil, garlic, parsley, clams, and water. Simmer until clams open, then combine with the scallop mixture. Add salt to taste.

Combine noodles with butter and cream and toss until blended.

Arrange noodles on a platter. Remove seafood mixture with slotted spoon and place on top of noodles. Sprinkle Parmesan cheese on top.

MAKES 4 SERVINGS

Photograph, Page 12

Dan McGrew's Restaurant & Saloon

400 S. Hartz Ave., Old Town Danville, CA 94526;
(415) 820-1800.

Dan McGrew's is like a chapter from the rip-roaring years of the turn of the century, when Robert Service penned his tales of the Yukon Gold rush, and weary sourdoughs could lift their spirits with the hearty food and good fellowship of the frontier saloons. At Dan McGrew's in Old Town Danville, guests dine amidst the nostalgic beauty of stained-glass chandeliers, a cozy fireplace, gold rush memorabilia, and the natural majesty of century-old redwood trees.

SALMON STUFFED MANICOTTI WITH MUSHROOM CREAM SAUCE

12 manicotti shells, preferably fresh
1 cup heavy cream
2 cups freshly grated Parmesan
  cheese
Salt and white pepper to taste
12 ounces fresh salmon, cooked
  and flaked
1¼ cups ricotta cheese
1 cup sliced mushrooms
Butter

In boiling salted water partially cook manicotti shells, approximately 5 minutes. Drain and allow to cool.

Mix cream and Parmesan cheese together and add salt and white pepper to taste. Set aside.

Blend together salmon and ricotta cheese to a soft paste. Fill a pastry bag with the salmon mixture and pipe to fill the manicotti.

Place stuffed manicotti in individual buttered baking dishes or 1 large casserole dish. Top with mushrooms and pour Parmesan mixture evenly over all. Refrigerate for at least 1 hour.

When ready to serve, bake at 400 degrees F. for 15 to 20 minutes or until hot and brown.

MAKES 4 SERVINGS

═POULTRY · EGGS═

Tam O'Shanter

2980 Los Feliz Blvd., Los Angeles, CA 90039;
(213) 664-0228.

Much of Los Angeles may be shimmering and new, but the Tam O'Shanter hearkens back to another era, when the city was still small, quiet, and unassuming. Now into its sixth decade, the Inn is the oldest restaurant in Los Angeles under the same ownership and in the same location. Although it has been remodeled and modernized through the years, care has been taken to retain the original quaint Scottish ambiance that charmed patrons way back in 1922.

HONEY GLAZED CHICKEN

1/4 cup honey
1/4 cup soy sauce
2 tablespoons sherry
1/4 cup salad oil
3 cloves garlic, crushed
1 tablespoon finely minced
   fresh ginger
4 whole chicken breasts

Combine honey, soy sauce, sherry, oil, garlic, and ginger in heavy-duty plastic bag. Rinse chicken and pat dry. Place in marinade in plastic bag and marinate overnight, turning occasionally if possible.

Remove chicken from marinade. Place in greased ovenproof dish and bake at 325 degrees F. for 60 minutes, or until golden brown.

MAKES 4 SERVINGS

Barragan's Irish Mexican Cafe

827 W. Glenoaks Blvd., Glendale, CA 91202;
(818) 240-3129.

Step off busy West Glenoaks Boulevard into the *muy simpatica* atmosphere of this excellent Mexican cafe. Under the loving guidance of owners Frank and Yolanda Barragan, the Cafe has become one of Glendale's most popular luncheon and dinner destinations for enchiladas, carnitas, and such house specialties as cocido soup, and the bountiful Barragan burritos, accompanied by frosty margaritas, and Mexican and American beers.

LISA MARIE BURRITO

Chicken Filling
2 medium tomatoes, chopped
1 1/2 medium onions, chopped
1 green pepper, chopped
3 tablespoons vegetable oil
1 pound cooked chicken,
  shredded
Salt and pepper to taste

Ranchero Sauce
3 medium tomatoes, chopped
1 1/2 medium onions, chopped
1 yellow chili pepper, chopped
2 tablespoons vegetable oil
1 teaspoon salt
3/8 teaspoon pepper
1/2 teaspoon granulated garlic
1 cup pureed whole tomato
1/2 cup water
1 (4-ounce) can whole Ortega
  brand chiles, cut lengthwise
  into strips
6 (10-inch or 12-inch) flour tortillas
1 pound Monterrey Jack cheese,
  grated

Garnish
Sour cream
Guacamole
Chopped green onions

To make chicken filling: In shallow frying pan saute tomatoes, onions, and pepper in oil, stirring occasionally, until limp. Add chicken and season with salt and pepper. Simmer on low heat 5 minutes. Set aside.

To make ranchero sauce: In another frying pan saute tomatoes, onion, and yellow chili in oil until limp. Season with salt, pepper, and garlic. Blend in pureed tomatoes and water, adding more if necessary. Bring to a boil, then add one-half of the chili strips. Reduce heat and simmer 5 minutes.

To make Burritos: Heat the chicken filling and divide it among the 6 tortillas placing it near the edge and mounding it slightly. Spoon 1 tablespoon ranchero sauce over each mound of chicken mixture. Fold opposite sides towards each other and roll the tortillas to encase the filling. Place burritos in a greased baking dish. Place remaining chili strips on top. Spoon remaining sauce over and top with cheese.

Place dish under broiler for 1 minute to melt cheese.

Garnish with sour cream, guacamole, or chopped green onions.

MAKES 6 SERVINGS
Photograph, Page 12

Anthony's

2509 Lakeshore Blvd., Lakeport, CA. 95453;
(707) 263-4905.

In a lovely natural setting by Clear Lake, California's largest lake, Anthony's is an intimate dinner house specializing in Italian regional cooking and American dishes prepared with a distinctive flair. In the elegant setting of red carpet, black velvet drapes, white lace tablecloths, hand-blown oil lamps, and an abundance of green plants, Anthony's staff proudly serves veal prepared eight imaginative ways. Lasagna, manicotti, and chicken oregano also attract diners from near and far away.

CHICKEN OREGANO

¾ cup vegetable oil
¼ cup lemon juice
3 tablespoons granulated garlic
  (not garlic salt)
3 tablespoons dried parsley
3 tablespoons dried oregano
1 tablespoon salt
1 teaspoon pepper
3 (2-pound) chickens, split in half

Combine oil, lemon juice, garlic, parsley, oregano, salt, and pepper in a large bowl.

Dip chicken in marinade and place skin side down, alternating legs so they fit into one another, in a 9-inch by 13-inch by 2-inch pan. Pour remaining marinade over chicken and cover tightly with foil.

Bake at 350 degrees F. for 1 hour.

Remove chicken from oven and let cool. Reserve marinade in refrigerator.

Refrigerate overnight, covered. Chicken will keep up to 4 days in refrigerator, or may be frozen.

When ready to serve, place chicken in shallow pan skin side down, pieces separated. Add marinade, which will be gelatinous. Broil until brown. Turn and broil skin side up until brown. Broil about 7 to 10 minutes on each side.

Serve with some of the marinade spooned over each chicken half.

MAKES 6 SERVINGS

Compass Rose

*The Westin St. Francis Hotel, Union Square,
335 Powell St., San Francisco, CA. 94102;
(415) 774-0167.*

The Compass Rose is one of San Francisco's truly grand restaurants and bars. Located in the prestigious old St. Francis Hotel, the Compass Rose, highlighted by richly carved wood paneling, ornate ceilings, and oriental artifacts, is reminiscent of a great San Francisco drawing room. This marvelous ambiance, with picture windows overlooking Powell and Geary Streets, is the perfect place to rendezvous for cocktails, a memorable luncheon or an invigorating afternoon tea.

SUPREME OF KAPON AU SAFFRON

2 tablespoons unsalted butter
1 tablespoon chopped shallots
Salt and pepper to taste
4 capon (see Glossary) breasts,
   skinned and boned
1 cup dry white wine
1 cup heavy cream
1/2 cup chicken stock (see Basic
   Stocks)
Pinch of saffron
3/4 pound spinach noodles,
   cooked
4 servings steamed fresh
   vegetables of the season
1 teaspoon chopped chives

Melt 1 tablespoon of butter in large oven-proof skillet and add shallots. Saute over medium heat for 2 minutes.

Salt and pepper capon breasts, add to skillet, and saute for 3 to 4 minutes on each side. Add wine to skillet and cook 1 minute.

Add cream, chicken stock, saffron, salt, and pepper. Cover and bake at 425 degrees F. for 15 minutes.

When capon is cooked, remove from skillet to warm platter. Place skillet over medium heat and reduce stock until it is slightly thick. Adjust seasoning to taste. Remove sauce from heat and whisk in the remaining tablespoon of butter.

Cover capon with sauce and serve with spinach noodles and vegetables sprinkled with chives.

MAKES 4 SERVINGS

O'neill's Continental Grill

2171 E. Rosecrans, El Segundo, CA 90245;
(213) 772-7818.

It took only a short time for O'Neill's to gather a faithful luncheon and dinner following among fans of the Hollywood Park Race Track and the Forum, and people doing business at the nearby Los Angeles International Airport. Under supervision of owner George Gialoumakis and executive chef Michael Guarnieri, O'Neill's specializes in steaks, chops, prime ribs, and fresh seafoods prepared on a mesquite wood broiler. The wine cellar offers a large selection of California and imported vintages at moderate prices.

CHICKEN O'NEILL

4 (10-ounce) boneless chicken
   breasts
1 (8-ounce) package cream cheese
1²/₃ cups chopped fresh spinach
Pinch of nutmeg
Salt and pepper to taste
¹/₄ teaspoon monosodium
   glutamate
Flour for dredging
¹/₂ cup clarified butter (see
   Glossary)

Remove skin from chicken breasts and pound meat with meat cleaver until ¹/₄ inch thick. Add salt and pepper.

In small bowl, combine cream cheese, chopped spinach, nutmeg, salt, pepper, and monosodium glutamate.

Shape ingredients into 4 cylinders. Roll each chicken breast around a cylinder and secure with a toothpick.

Dredge in flour and saute in butter over medium heat for 3 minutes on each side.

Place in a greased casserole and bake at 350 degrees F. for 10 to 15 minutes or until done.

MAKES 4 SERVINGS

515 S. Flower St., Level C, Los Angeles, CA 90071;
(213) 629-2565.

O'Shaughnessey's Downtown is a delightful blend of the old world and the new, the traditional and the unexpected, which adds up to a fun place to wine and dine. American through and through, O'Shaughnessey's also offers a warm, castle-like atmosphere, with stone walls, massive ironwork chandeliers, big fireplaces, and soft, romantic candlelight. The menu ranges from steaks and fresh seafoods to such surprises as buffalo stew, buffalo steaks, rabbit, and quail.

BREAST OF CHICKEN WELLINGTON

Mushroom Puree
4 teaspoons finely minced shallots
2 cups finely chopped mushrooms
4 teaspoons clarified butter (see
* Glossary)*
4 teaspoons flour
8 tablespoons heavy cream
4 teaspoons lemon juice
Salt and pepper to taste

Chicken Wellington
4 (6-ounce) boned chicken breasts
Salt and white pepper to taste
Flour for dredging
8 tablespoons clarified butter,
* melted (see Glossary)*
8 tablespoons liver pâté
4 (6-inch by 6-inch) squares puff
* pastry dough (available in*
* frozen food section of*
* grocery stores)*
4 egg yolks
4 tablespoons water

To make mushroom puree: In small saucepan, saute shallots and mushrooms over high heat, but do not brown. Add flour and stir, using a wooden spoon. Stir in cream and boil for 5 minutes or until it has the consistency of thick cream of wheat. Season with lemon juice, salt, and pepper and cool.

To make Chicken Wellington: Season chicken with salt and white pepper. Dredge in flour, then saute over medium heat in butter for 3 minutes on each side until golden. Chill for 20 minutes.

Place 2 tablespoons mushroom puree on top of each chicken breast, then 2 slices of liver pâté. Lay dough square on top of chicken and fold neatly under, into the shape of a tennis ball. Brush with 1 egg yolk mixed with 1 tablespoon water. Place on slightly oiled baking sheet and bake at 350 degrees F. for approximately 30 minutes.

MAKES 4 SERVINGS

El Torito

13715 Fiji Way, Marina del Rey, CA 90292;
(213) 823-8941.

Thirty years ago, even those few Americans who did know anything about Mexican food usually thought of it in terms no more exciting than tacos and refried beans. That's when Larry J. Cano opened the first El Torito Restaurant and introduced a dulled American palate to such tangy new taste sensations as chimichangas, enchiladas suizas, deep-fried ice cream, and deep-fried tortillas in an elegant fan-shaped shell. El Torito was also an innovator in the Margarita field.

ENCHILADAS SUIZAS

Chicken Filling
2 tablespoons vegetable oil
1/2 medium onion, sliced
1 clove garlic, crushed
1 Pasilla chile pepper, roasted, peeled, and sliced
1 tomato, chopped
1/2 cup tomato sauce (see Basic Sauces)
1 1/4 cups chicken stock (see Basic Stocks)
1/2 teaspoon salt
1/8 teaspoon white pepper
1/8 teaspoon granulated garlic
Pinch of cumin
1 1/2 cups shredded cooked chicken

Salsa Verde
1/2 cup vegetable oil
6 tablespoons chopped green pepper
1/2 medium onion, sliced
1 garlic clove, finely minced
2 cups chicken stock
2 green chile peppers, roasted, peeled, and sliced
2 tablespoons chopped cilantro (see Glossary)

To make chicken filling: In medium pan heat oil and add onions and garlic. Cook over medium heat, stirring, 3 to 4 minutes. Add chile, tomato, tomato sauce, and chicken stock. Simmer about 5 minutes. Add salt, pepper, garlic, cumin, and chicken. Simmer about 5 minutes. Set aside to cool.

To make salsa verde: In medium pan heat 1/4 cup of oil and add green pepper, onion, and garlic. Cook over medium heat, stirring, about 3 to 4 minutes. Add chicken stock and set aside.

In blender or food processor combine until smooth green chiles, cilantro, vinegar, and tomatillo. Add to vegetables and simmer for about 5 minutes. Add salt, pepper, garlic, and cumin.

In separate small skillet heat remaining 1/4 cup of oil. Add flour and cook, stirring until mixture is light brown. Do not overcook. Add to sauce mixture and simmer about 5 minutes.

ENCHILADAS SUIZAS (Continued)

1 tablespoon white vinegar
1 tomatillo (available in Latin
   markets)
$1/4$ teaspoon salt
$1/8$ teaspoon white pepper
$1/8$ teaspoon granulated garlic
$1/4$ teaspoon cumin
5 tablespoons flour

Enchiladas
Oil for frying
8 corn tortillas
4 ounces Monterrey Jack cheese,
   shredded
4 ounces Cheddar cheese,
   shredded
1 cup sour cream

To make enchiladas: Heat 2 inches of oil in medium skillet. Dip tortillas in hot oil about 30 seconds on each side. Remove and drain on paper towels.

Fill each tortilla with 3 tablespoons chicken filling and 1 tablespoon Monterrey and Cheddar cheeses combined. Roll and place in 9-inch by 13-inch ovenproof casserole. Repeat this process for all 8 tortillas.

Top enchiladas with salsa verde and sprinkle with remaining cheese. Bake at 350 degrees F. for 20 minutes or until cheese is melted and bubbly.

Serve enchiladas with sour cream.

MAKES 4 SERVINGS

Miyako

139 S. Los Robles Ave., Pasadena, CA 91101;
(818) 795-7005.

Sukiyaki, a delicious tradition at Miyako Restaurants, comes from ancient Japan, where farmers, at the end of their long day in the fields, would prepare their dinner by roasting meat and vegetables on a plowshare over an open fire. Today, at Miyako Restaurants in Pasadena, Orange, and Torrance, sukiyaki's harmonious blend of vegetables, choice beef, rice wine and special sauce is prepared at your table in a sizzling pan. Golden-fried tempura and teriyaki are other Miyako hallmarks.

TEMPURA

Tempura Sauce
2 cups cold water
1 teaspoon Hondashi (Japanese soup base available in oriental markets)
1/2 cup Japanese soy sauce
1 tablespoon sugar
2 tablespoons sake (Japanese wine)

Tempura Batter
2 yolks from medium eggs
2 cups cold water
2 cups flour
1/4 teaspoon baking powder

Chicken
Fish and shellfish
Vegetables, such as brocolli, green peppers, carrots, onions
Oil for deep-frying

To make tempura sauce: Place all ingredients in saucepan and bring to a boil. Turn off heat.

To make tempura batter: Beat egg yolks with water. Combine egg-water mixture with flour and baking powder just before using. Do not stir too much, and do not worry if the batter is uneven and lumpy.

A variety of chicken, fish, and vegetables may be selected for frying. Cut each item artistically into bite-size portions. Thoroughly coat each item in batter and deep-fry in oil at 350 degrees F. until golden brown.

Serve with tempura sauce for dipping.

MAKES 4 SERVINGS

The Cat & The Custard Cup

800 E. Whittier Blvd., La Habra, CA 90631;
(213) 694-3812.

Amid the splendor of old brick, polished woods, warm fireplaces, and copper pots, The Cat & The Custard Cup invites the weary to refresh their spirits with veal joints, baby salmon, roast filet mignon, salads, and hearty soups, accompanied by British and American ales and beers, wines, and cocktails. After a brief sojourn in these friendly rooms, you'll swear you've been magically transported back to Olde London town.

AYLESBURY DUCKLING

1 (4½-pound to 5-pound)
   duck
1 cup duck or chicken stock (see
   Basic Stocks)
2 tablespoons currant jelly
1 teaspoon sherry
Dash of Worcestershire sauce
Pinch of salt and white pepper
2 teaspoons sugar
⅛ teaspoon caramel
⅛ teaspoon red food coloring
1 teaspoon brandy
1 tablespoon arrowroot (see
   Glossary) mixed in 6
   tablespoons cold water

Place duck in roasting pan and roast at 375 degrees F. for 1 hour, turning every 15 minutes to brown all sides evenly. Drain fat as needed.

While duck is cooking, combine in saucepan stock, currant jelly, sherry, Worcestershire, salt, pepper, sugar, caramel, and food coloring.

Cook sauce over moderate heat until hot and jelly is melted. Stir occasionally. Add brandy and arrowroot and stir to thicken. Do not boil.

Remove duck from pan and cut in half. Pour sauce over each half and serve.

MAKES 2 SERVINGS

Photograph, Page 9

Chez Cary

571 S. Main St., Orange, CA 92668;
(714) 542-3595.

Crevettes sur glace...potage escargots...ris de veau financiere...cotes d' agneau vert...scampis a la francaise...pear belle Helene. The menu at Chez Cary reads like a gourmet's wish-book, and the only agony is trying to decide which of these many lovely dishes to enjoy. Choosing the right setting can also be a delightful dilemma. Will it be the main dining room, with its gleaming crystal and candlelight, or the Wine Cellar, a unique venue for gourmet dining that seats 12 in privacy and Old World charm?

DUCK A LA APRICOT

Ducks
3 ducks
Salt and white pepper to taste
1 tablespoon rosemary
1 cup honey

Apricot Sauce
1 cup chopped onion
1 cup chopped carrots
1 cup chopped celery
1 (8-ounce) can tomato puree
2 cups red wine
2 quarts chicken stock (see Basic
    Stocks)
3 bay leaves
1 tablespoon rosemary
1 teaspoon whole black
    peppercorns
2 cups sugar
2 cups dry sherry
1/2 cup apricot marmalade
1 (16-ounce) can apricot halves
3 tablespoons cornstarch,
    dissolved in 1/4 cup red wine
Pinch of ground cinnamon
Pinch of ground rosemary
Pinch of ground cloves
Salt and white pepper to taste
1 teaspoon red wine vinegar
1/2 teaspoon Kitchen Bouquet (see
    Glossary)
2 tablespoons apricot brandy

To cook ducks: Remove giblets from ducks and reserve for sauce. Cut off wing tips. Add salt, pepper, and rosemary to inside cavity of duck. Tie wings and legs to body with string.

Salt and pepper outside and roast at 475 degrees F. for 1 hour, turning every 20 minutes so that all sides are roasted evenly, draining grease as necessary, and basting occasionally.

When ducks are well-browned on all sides, drain grease and allow ducks to cool. Refrigerate overnight.

To make apricot sauce: Make a stock by placing giblets (except livers), necks, and wing tips in a roasting pan and cook uncovered at 350 degrees F. until golden brown.

Add chopped onions, celery, and carrots. Roast another 20 to 30 minutes. Add tomato puree and red wine. Cook until almost dry.

Then add chicken stock, bay leaves, rosemary, and peppercorns, and cook on top of the stove over medium heat for 2 hours.

Strain stock and discard bones and vegetables. Skim off grease and set stock aside.

In saucepan heat sugar and stir over moderate heat until it melts and carmelizes to dark brown. Do not burn. When sugar is carmelized, remove from heat and add sherry, stirring well.

Add apricot marmalade and canned apricots with syrup. Cook and reduce two-thirds.

Then add duck stock, boil for 1 1/2 hours slowly, over moderate heat, stirring occasionally.

DUCK A LA APRICOT (Continued)

Add dissolved cornstarch mixture, bring to boil, and cook until thickened. Cook for another hour, stirring occasionally.

Add cinnamon, rosemary, cloves, salt, white pepper, vinegar and Kitchen Bouquet. Just before serving stir in apricot brandy.

To serve, cut ducks in half and heat at 350 degrees F. for 20 minutes or until warm. Brush skin side of ducks with honey and place under broiler until skin is brown and crisp, about 3 minutes. Place duck half on serving platter and spoon warm sauce over.

MAKES 6 SERVINGS

The Cliff House

1090 Point Lobos, at Seal Rocks, San Francisco, CA 94121; (415) 387-5847.

What more fitting way to conclude a visit to San Francisco's famed Seal Rocks than a spectacular sunset, great cocktails, wines, and dinner at The Cliff House? The Cliff House offers two dining venues, both with ocean views. The Seafood & Beverage Co. specializes in fresh seafoods, burgers, chicken, ribs, and desserts. Its companion, Upstairs, counters with 45 styles of omelettes, soups, salads, gourmet sandwiches, pasta, quiche, seafood, and ribs.

EGGS SAN FRANCISCO

10 eggs, poached

Sauce
3 tablespoons butter
2 tablespoons finely chopped onions
3 tablespoons flour
1 1/2 cups milk
2 tablespoons brandy
1 teaspoon strained fresh lemon juice
1/8 teaspoon cayenne pepper
1 teaspoon salt

Crabmeat
6 tablespoons butter
1 pound crabmeat
1/8 teaspoon cayenne pepper
1/2 teaspoon salt

Garnish
Bits of butter
Paprika

To poach eggs: Crack eggs into a pan of simmering water large enough and deep enough to cover eggs. When cooked to desired degree of doneness, remove from water with a slotted spoon and place in a bowl of cold water to stop the cooking. To reheat place eggs back in simmering water until heated through.

To make sauce: Melt butter over moderate heat. When foam begins to subside, add onions and, stirring frequently, cook for about 5 minutes or until they are soft and translucent, but not brown. Add flour and mix well, stirring constantly with wire whisk. Pour in milk in a slow thin stream and cook over high heat until sauce comes to a boil, thickens, and is smooth. Reduce heat to low and simmer uncovered for 2 or 3 minutes.

In small pan, heat brandy over low heat and ignite it, then slide pan back and forth gently until flames die. Stir brandy, lemon juice, cayenne pepper, and salt into the sauce, and taste for seasoning. Remove from heat and cover to keep warm until ready to use.

To prepare crabmeat: In heavy skillet melt butter over moderate heat. Add crabmeat and toss gently until hot and evenly moistened. Stir in cayenne and salt. Cover with foil to keep warm.

To assemble: Divide crabmeat onto 5 ovenproof plates. Arrange 2 warm poached eggs per serving on the crabmeat. Spoon brandied cream sauce over the eggs and sprinkle the top with butter bits and paprika. Bake at 450 degrees F. for 10 minutes, or until top is golden brown.

MAKES 5 SERVINGS

SEAFOOD

Rosebud's English Pub

370 Geary St., San Francisco, CA 94102;
(415) 433-0183.

In the heart of San Francisco's Theatre Row, only a block from busy Union Square, Rosebud's might just as well be at Leicester Square in London. With its authentic English pub decor — rich wood paneling, tapestry wall coverings, and serving staff in proper English costume — Rosebud's is famous for its roasted prime ribs of beef with Yorkshire pudding, as well as California seafoods, beef, chicken, and duckling dishes.

PRAWNS AMARETTO

24 large prawns, peeled and
*   deveined (see Glossary)*
Flour for dredging
1/3 cup butter
4 teaspoons grated orange rind
1/2 cup orange juice
1/2 cup white wine
1/2 cup brandy
1 cup heavy cream
1/2 cup Amaretto
Salt and pepper to taste
4 slices of white toast, trimmed and
*   halved*

Garnish
Chopped parsley

Flour prawns and saute over medium heat in butter, stirring until light brown, about 3 minutes.

Add orange rind, orange juice, wine, brandy, and cream and stir to make a sauce. Add Amaretto and salt and pepper to taste.

To serve, place prawns on top of toast halves, pour sauce over, and garnish with chopped parsley.

MAKES 4 SERVINGS

Spindrifter

3333 W. Coast Hwy., Newport Beach, CA 92660;
(714) 642-2295.

Off the scenic Pacific Coast Highway, overlooking the boats in picturesque Newport Harbor, The Spindrifter invites guests into an intimate and thoroughly comfortable setting for the enjoyment of some of California's finest seafoods. Skillfully prepared veal dishes, steaks, fowl, a memorable prime rib, and an elegant Sunday Champagne Brunch also attract appreciative diners. There is nightly entertainment and boaters may tie up at The Spindrifter's private dock.

BAKED STUFFED SHRIMP

20 slices bacon
3/4 cup diced onion
1/2 cup diced green pepper
1/2 cup butter
3/4 cup cooked coarsely
    chopped tiny shrimp
1/4 cup Hollandaise sauce (see
    Basic Sauces)
1 teaspoon salt
1/4 teaspoon pepper
1 cup fresh bread crumbs
20 jumbo shrimp

Blanch bacon in boiling water for 3 minutes. Drain and set aside.

Saute onion and pepper in butter over medium heat until soft, about 8 minutes. Add tiny shrimp, Hollandaise, salt, and pepper. Heat without boiling, and add bread crumbs to thicken stuffing.

Shell jumbo shrimp leaving tails on. Devein and butterfly by cutting down the back without cutting through completely. Place 1/8 cup stuffing on back of each shrimp and wrap with 1 thin slice of bacon. Bake at 350 degrees F. for approximately 10 minutes. Place tails facing edge of plate.

Serve with sauteed vegetables and rice pilaf, fettucini alfredo, or a stuffed baked potato. Toasted garlic cheese bread adds a nice touch.

MAKES 4 SERVINGS

Photograph, Page 12

The Cliff House

1090 Point Lobos, at Seal Rocks, San Francisco, CA 94121; (415) 386-3330.

The Cliff House at San Francisco's dramatic Seal Rocks has been a tradition since the Gold Rush days of the 1850s. There are actually two restaurants in one at Cliff House: Seafood & Beverage Co., featuring fresh seafoods and other luncheon and dinner fare; and Upstairs, offering a choice of 45 omelettes, soups and salads throughout the day, and pasta and seafood dishes at dinner. From either, the views of Ocean Beach, Pacific sunsets, and ocean traffic are inspiring.

CREVETTES "MARGARITA" (Shrimp with Tequila)

20 shrimp, peeled and deveined
  (see Glossary)
4 teaspoons lime juice
Salt and pepper to taste
2 ripe avocados, peeled
1/2 cup butter
1/4 cup finely chopped shallots
1/2 cup tequila
1 cup heavy cream
1/4 cup finely chopped cilantro (see
  Glossary)

Cut shrimp along back side to open or butterfly. Do not cut completely through. Place in bowl and add lime juice, salt, and pepper. Let stand briefly until time to cook.

Cut avocado into 1/2-inch slices.

Heat butter over medium heat in skillet; add shrimp, stirring rapidly and cook about 2 minutes. Sprinkle with shallots and cook, stirring, about 10 seconds. Add tequila.

Increase heat and add cream. Cook over high heat about 1 minute. Add salt and pepper to taste. Add avocado slices and cook only until slices are hot, no longer. Using a slotted spoon, transfer shrimp and avocado to hot serving dishes.

Bring sauce to a full rolling boil for about 30 seconds and add chopped cilantro. Spoon sauce over the shrimp and avocado.

MAKES 4 SERVINGS

The Cliff House

1090 Point Lobos, at Seals Rocks, San Francisco, CA 94121; (415) 386-3330.

The Seafood & Beverage Co.'s name says it all. One of two excellent dining experiences at the Cliff House at San Francisco's Seal Rocks, this cheerful restaurant specializes in such delicacies as sole, calamari, Dungeness crab, shrimp, oysters, red snapper, and always a fresh catch-of-the-day. For variety's sake, great burgers, ribs, steaks, chicken, and luscious desserts are also served. All this, and guests have incomparable views of Seal Rocks, Ocean Beach, and the bi-annual whale migrations.

LOBSTER THERMIDOR

3 quarts fish stock (see Basic
   Stocks)
1 lobster
2 tablespoons butter
¼ teaspoon dry mustard
¼ teaspoon salt
¼ teaspoon pepper
2 shallots
¼ cup finely chopped onion
1 small bay leaf
1 clove garlic, finely chopped
¼ cup white wine
1 cup half and half
½ cup white sauce (see Basic
   Sauces)
3 ounces cheddar cheese, grated

Bring fish stock to boil. Place live lobster in boiling stock, cover, and cook for 10 minutes.

Remove lobster, cut in half, and remove claws. Remove all the meat from the claws and body, reserving the 2 halves of the shell. Finely dice meat.

Melt butter in skillet over medium heat. Add mustard, salt, pepper, shallots, onion, bay leaf, and garlic and saute, stirring, for about 5 minutes.

Add wine, half and half, white sauce, and lobster. Bring to a boil. Remove immediately from heat.

Fill lobster shells with mixture, sprinkle grated cheese on top, and place under broiler for 1 to 2 minutes.

MAKES 2 SERVINGS

Acapulco y Los Arcos

Thirty-One California Locations

Anyone laboring under the misconception that all Mexican food is a chili-laden three-alarm fire is in for a delicious revelation at an Acapulco Restaurant. Since opening his first Mexican restaurant in Pasadena in 1961, founder Ray Marshall has dedicated his waking hours to the development of this wonderful cuisine. His many creations include the crabmeat enchilada for which he won the Gold Medal at the San Francisco Crab Olympics, and Vista Del Mar, an incredible marriage of shrimp, chicken breast, crabmeat, and avocado. The margaritas are also an art in their own right.

CRAB ENCHILADA (The San Francisco Special)

Salas con Tomatillos
1 (12-ounce) can tomatillos (see Note)
2 tortillas
Oil or lard for frying
1/4 cup chopped onion
1 fresh chile (jalapeno or querito)
1 tablespoon chopped cilantro (see Glossary)
1/2 teaspoon chopped garlic
1/2 teaspoon salt
1/2 cup water or chicken stock (see Basic Stocks)
1/4 teaspoon sugar
3 drops green food coloring

Crab Enchilada
6 corn tortillas
Oil or lard for heating
1 1/2 cups crabmeat sauteed in butter
6 tablespoons minced onion
Shredded Monterrey Jack cheese
Sour cream

Garnish
Pitted ripe olives
Avocado slices
Tomatoes, peeled and sliced

To make salsa con tomatillos: Drain tomatillos, reserving liquid. Fry 2 tortillas in oil or fat until lightly browned and break into the juice of the tomatillos in order to soften.

Heat oil and saute onion, chile, cilantro, garlic, and salt until soft but not browned. Put tomatillos, softened tortillas, and juice, sauteed mixture, stock or water, sugar and food coloring into a blender or food processor and process until smooth.

Sauce may be used as is or strained for a smoother presentation

To make crab enchilada: Heat tortillas in oil or lard until soft.

Place 1/4 cup crab meat in center of each, then sprinkle with 1 tablespoon onion. Spoon a little salsa con tomatillos on each. Roll enchilada and place in shallow pan seam side down. Cover with remaining salsa con tomatillos. Sprinkle generously with shredded cheese and bake at 400 degrees F. about 10 minutes or until hot and cheese is melted.

Serve with a dollop of sour cream and garnish with olives, avocado, and tomato slices.

Note: Canned tomatillos (Mexican tomatoes) are available in the Mexican section of most markets.

MAKES 6 SERVINGS

Dan McGrew's Restaurant & Saloon

400 S. Hartz Ave., Old Town Danville, CA 94526; (415) 820-1800.

Even the ornery Dangerous Dan McGrew himself most likely would take a shine to civilized ways again after a lunch or dinner at Dan McGrew's in Old Town Danville. One of the most vivid and memorable characters from author Robert Service's chronicles of the Yukon Gold Rush in the 19th century, Dangerous Dan has inspired this warm, hospitable retreat where great food, hearty drinks, and fellowship are hallmarks.

BROILED FRESH HALIBUT
WITH AVOCADO SAUCE AND SALSA PIQUANTE

Avocado Sauce
1 avocado
2 tablespoons minced onion
1/4 cup olive oil
Juice of 1 lemon
Salt and white pepper to taste

Salsa Piquante
4 tomatoes, peeled, seeded,
   and diced
2 tablespoons finely minced
   red onion
1 green chile, minced
Dash of Tobasco
Dash of Worcestershire sauce
1 clove garlic, minced
1 tablespoon finely chopped
   cilantro (see Glossary)
Pinch of oregano
Pinch of basil
Salt and white pepper to taste

8 halibut steaks
Olive oil

Garnish
Lemon slices
Chopped fresh cilantro

To make avocado sauce: Put avocado, onion, olive oil, lemon juice, salt, and pepper into blender or food processor and process to puree. Keep at room temperature.

To make salsa piquante: Combine tomatoes, onions, pepper, Tobasco, Worcestershire sauce, garlic, cilantro, oregano, basil, salt, and pepper in bowl. Keep at room temperature.

To cook halibut: Brush halibut steaks with olive oil and broil until fish flakes when tested with a fork. Serve with room temperature sauces placed side by side on top of fish.

Garnish with lemon and chopped fresh cilantro.

MAKES 8 SERVINGS

Francois'

Arco Plaza, 555 S. Flower St., Los Angeles, CA 90071; (213) 680-2727.

Patrons of the Hollywood Bowl and the Greek Theatre, and those who want to enjoy a classy picnic in a park or on their own patios, often rely on the talented staff at Francois' for just the right touch of gourmet excellence. Francois' picnic dinners come in attractive rattan hampers and include an appetizer, choice of entree, marinated vegetables, imported cheeses, freshly baked breads, fruit, a luscious Francois' pastry, after dinner mints, and all the necessary utensils and condiments.

PAPILLOTE OF SALMON

1/2 cup carrots, julienned (see
    Glossary)
1/2 cup celery, julienned
1/2 cup mushrooms, julienned
1/2 cup leeks, julienned
1/2 cup unsalted butter
Parchment paper
4 (6-ounce) salmon steaks,
    skin removed
Salt and white pepper to taste
4 tablespoons white wine
1/2 teaspoon finely chopped
    shallots
Juice of 2 lemons
1 cube chicken bouillon

Lightly saute julienned vegetables over moderate heat in 4 teaspoons of butter for 2 minutes. Vegetables should remain crisp.

Cut 4 sheets parchment paper in heart shapes much larger than salmon. Rub a little butter on 1 side of the paper, about the size of the fish. On top, place the cooked vegetables.

Cut salmon lengthwise into 4 slices, place on top of the vegetables, and season with salt and pepper. Put shallots on top and pour white wine over. Crumble remaining pieces of butter on top and pour lemon juice over. For final topping, crumble chicken bouillon cube evenly over all.

Fold paper over in half. then crimp edges of paper tightly together to seal. Place on baking sheet and bake at 425 degrees F. for 8 or 9 minutes or until paper puffs up.

Serve immediately. When serving, slit paper down the middle and remove fish, vegetables, and sauce to a serving plate.

MAKES 4 SERVINGS

At Marty's

8657 W. Pico Blvd., Los Angeles, CA. 90035;
(213) 272-1048.

The setting is so enchanting that many a patron stops by At Marty's just to linger over a cocktail, a glass of wine, or a delicious dessert and coffee while letting their eyes play over the Art Deco fantasy of mirrors, sculpted glass, and statuary. To be sure, a great many stay on, to savor the joys of At Marty's delectable cuisine. After such delights as emerald sea bass, paella, veal Nubita, and lychee chicken, they go out the doors whistling, " 'S Wonderful, 'S Marvelous."

EMERALD SEA BASS

Pesto
5 (10-ounce) packages frozen
   chopped spinach
3 cups butter, melted
3 shallots
8 cloves garlic or 4 tablespoons
   granulated garlic
1/2 teaspoon black pepper
1 teaspoon salt
20 capers, drained

Sea Bass
4 sea bass fillets

Garnish
Pimiento
Additional capers

To prepare pesto: Cook spinach in skillet only until thawed. Drain and squeeze all moisture from spinach.

Combine spinach and butter in blender or food processor and blend until thick and fine. Do this in batches, if necessary. Place in large bowl.

Blend shallots, garlic, pepper, salt, and capers in blender or food processor. Add to the spinach mixture and mix well with a wire whisk. Refrigerate until solid.

To prepare sea bass: When ready to cook, place two-thirds of pesto in bottom of ovenproof dish. Place fish on pesto and top with remaining pesto.

Bake at 400 degrees F. for 10 to 12 minutes. Remove to serving platter and garnish with pimiento and additional capers.

Note: Shrimp or other seafood may be substituted for bass. This dish goes well with most varieties of pasta.

MAKES 4 SERVINGS

Poor Richard's Kitchen

1198 S. Coast Hwy., Laguna Beach, CA 92651;
(714) 497-1667.

Poor Richard's Kitchen is on the top level of the Village Fair Mall, and offers spectacular Pacific Ocean views and relaxed outdoor patio dining. Operated for more than six years by Richard Stenger and Myron Ross, this delightful place is a popular retreat for a breakfast of Belgian waffles and omelettes, and luncheon and dinner that range from soups and salads to New Orleans-style seafood gumbo, Alaskan halibut steaks, fresh seafoods, sirloin and filet mignon steaks.

POOR RICHARD'S BOUILLABAISSE

1 medium onion, diced
2 leeks, sliced
2 cloves garlic, chopped
1/2 cup butter
3 cups chicken stock (see Basic Stocks)
1 cup white wine
1 (28-ounce) can chopped tomatoes
2 bay leaves
1 teaspoon thyme
1 teaspoon saffron
1 teaspoon Pernod (see Glossary)
1 cup frozen English peas
1 pound snow crab in shell
1 pound cod or sea bass, cut in bite-size pieces
12 medium shrimp, peeled and deveined (see Glossary)
12 medium scallops
12 clams in shells
Salt and cayenne pepper to taste

In skillet lightly saute onion, leeks, and garlic in butter over medium heat, stirring, until onions are transparent, about 5 to 7 minutes.

Add chicken stock, wine, tomatoes, bay leaves, thyme, and saffron and bring to a boil.

Add Pernod, peas, crab, fish, shrimp, and scallops. Cover pot and simmer 10 to 15 minutes; do not stir.

Add clams and simmer until shells open, 10 to 15 minutes more. Season with salt and cayenne to taste.

Serve with sourdough garlic toast.

MAKES 6 SERVINGS

Twenty-Six Locations in California.

The 26 Hungry Tiger restaurants have a proud heritage. The original, on Ventura Boulevard in Sherman Oaks, was opened in 1962 by Bob Prescott, a member of the famed World War II flying team, the Flying Tigers. Prescott also founded Flying Tiger Airlines, and thus was able to fly Maine lobsters to his West Coast restaurants daily. The Tigers pride themselves on being a non-chain chain, with each restaurant reflecting the character and mood of its individual location.

HUNGRY TIGER BOUILLABAISSE

1 cup diced onion
1 cup diced celery
1 cup diced leek
1 cup diced tomato, peeled
   and seeded
¼ cup olive oil
¼ cup sauterne wine
¼ cup dry sherry
1 tablespoon Pernod (see Glossary)
1 (6-ounce) can tomato puree
2 quarts rich fish stock (see Basic
   Stocks)
2 tablespoons fennel seeds
Pinch of saffron
Salt and white pepper to taste
3 (1-pound) Maine lobsters, split
   and cut in 4 pieces
12 large shrimp in shells
1 pound Halibut steak, cut in
   bite-size pieces (or other
   fresh fish)
1 pound Pacific red snapper, cut in
   bite-size pieces, or other
   fresh fish
1 pound Alaskan crab in shell, split
12 little neck clams in shells
6 to 8 mussels in shells (optional)

Saute onion, celery, leek, and tomato in olive oil over medium heat, stirring occasionally, until soft, about 7 to 9 minutes. Add sauterne and sherry and reduce by one-third.

Add Pernod, tomato puree, fish stock, fennel seeds, saffron, salt, and pepper and simmer 1 hour.

Add lobsters, shrimp, fish, crab, clams, and mussels to sauce and cook until fish is done and clams and mussels are open, about 15 minutes. Serve family style with a green salad and garlic toast.

MAKES 6 TO 8 SERVINGS

Photograph, Page 11

2400 Lombard St., San Francisco, CA 94123;
(415) 563-8988

Scott's Seafood Grill & Bar is reminiscent of Old San Francisco with all the accessories of turn-of-the-century life in the bay city. Prints of this earlier time decorate the walls and Oriental rugs cover the dark polished floors. Scott's is a comfortable seafood house and popular bar in the area, where cheerful company and fresh seafare are guaranteed.

CIOPPINO

Marinara Sauce
1/2 cup olive oil
2 cups coarsely chopped onion
1/3 cup grated carrot
2 cloves garlic, finely minced
4 cups canned tomatoes
Salt and pepper to taste
1/4 cup butter
1 teaspoon oregano
1 teaspoon basil

Cioppino
1 cup sliced mushrooms
1 pound fish cut in bite-size pieces
8 prawns, peeled and deveined
16 scallops
2 garlic cloves, finely chopped
2 shallots, finely chopped
4 cups fish stock (see Basic Stocks)
1 cup white wine
6 clams in shells
4 ounces peeled, raw shrimp
4 ounces crabmeat

Garnish
Chopped parsley

To make Marinara Sauce: Heat oil in skillet and add onion, carrot, and garlic. Cook over moderate heat, stirring, until vegetables are golden brown.

Puree tomatoes in a blender or food processor and strain. Add tomato pulp to the vegetables. Season with salt and pepper, partially cover, and simmer 15 minutes. Strain sauce, pushing as many solids through strainer as possible.

Return to skillet, add butter, oregano, and basil. Partially cover and simmer 30 minutes longer. Makes 3 to 4 cups marinara sauce.

To prepare Cioppino: In large pot combine mushrooms, fish, prawns, scallops, garlic, shallots, fish stock, wine, and clams. Cover and simmer over medium heat for 10 minutes or until fish is done. Add 2 cups marinara sauce, shrimp, and crabmeat and simmer until shrimp are cooked, about 5 minutes.

Divide among 4 soup bowls placing clams and prawns on top of the stew. Garnish with chopped parsley and serve with French bread.

MAKES 4 SERVINGS

DESSERTS

Anaheim Marriott Hotel, 700 W. Convention Way,
Anaheim, CA 92802;
(714) 750-8000.

A lovely retreat inside the deluxe Anaheim Marriott Hotel, JW's takes great pride in its impeccably prepared nouvelle cuisine. Inspired by the classical cooking of France, JW's menu stresses the freshest ingredients, with light, delicate sauces, accented by bouquets of vegetables, salads, soups, and desserts. Adding to the romance and elegance, the sounds of a harp fill the dining room. JW's extensive wine list includes premium vintages from California, Germany, Italy, and France.

SACHER TORTE

Torte
3/4 cup all purpose flour
5 ounces semi-sweet chocolate
10 tablespoons soft butter
1 cup confectioners' sugar
6 eggs, separated
1 cup apricot jam, heated

Chocolate Icing
4 ounces semi-sweet chocolate
3/4 cup confectioners' sugar
1/4 cup water
1 drop quality olive oil

Garnish
Whipped cream

To make torte: Sift flour twice and set aside.

Melt chocolate in double boiler and allow to cool.

Mix together butter with 3/4 cup sugar. Add egg yolks rapidly. Add cooled melted chocolate and stir well.

Whip egg whites until stiff. Whisk in remaining 1/4 cup sugar. Fold egg whites and flour alternately into butter-chocolate mixture.

Pour into buttered and floured 9-inch cake pan and bake at 350 degrees F. approximately 50 to 60 minutes. Let inverted cake cool on rack for 1 hour. Slice horizontally through the middle and spread with warm apricot jam. Place other half of cake on top.

To make chocolate icing: Melt chocolate over simmering water in double boiler. In saucepan dissolve sugar in water, and cook to 230 to 234 degrees F. Remove from heat and allow to cool. Stir lukewarm sugar solution into melted chocolate; add drop of olive oil. Stir constantly until mixture has thickened sufficiently to spread over cake.

Spread chocolate icing on cake and garnish with whipped cream.

MAKES 8 SERVINGS

Vickman's

1228 E. Eighth St., Los Angeles, CA 90021;
(213) 622-3852.

Breakfast and lunch at Vickman's has been a cherished Los Angeles tradition since 1930. Many Angelenos combine a tasty meal at Vickman's with a trip to the nearby Produce Market, the Flower Market, and bargain-hunting forays into the Garment District. Breakfast offers a tempting selection of freshly-baked Danish pastries, fresh fruit, and the renowned Market Omelette. Lunch is highlighted by a variety of hefty sandwiches, salads, and daily hot specials.

VICKMAN'S FRESH STRAWBERRY PIE

Pie Pastry
1 cup all purpose flour
1/4 teaspoon salt
1/4 cup butter, chilled
3 tablespoons vegetable
  shortening, chilled
2 to 6 tablespoons ice water

Pie Filling
2 cups sugar
2 cups water
3 tablespoons cornstarch,
  dissolved in 1/4 cup water
Red food coloring
1 quart fresh strawberries
1 pint heavy cream, whipped

To make pie pastry: Sift flour and salt together into bowl. Using pastry blender cut in butter and shortening until mixture is the size of small peas. Sprinkle on water, 1 tablespoon at a time, tossing mixture with pastry blender or a fork. When mixture holds together when pinched between thumb and forefinger, stop adding water.

Gather mixture into a ball and turn out onto floured surface. Continue forming into a ball and roll with floured rolling pin to desired size. Makes 1 pie crust.

To make pie filling: Place sugar and water in saucepan, mix well, and bring to a boil. Add cornstarch mixture to boiling sugar and water, stirring rapidly until mixture is clear. Add few drops of red color, stir, and set glaze aside to cool.

Remove stems from strawberries and clean by gently rolling back and forth in a clean dry cloth. Spoon 1/2 inch of glaze in bottom of baked pie crust. Cover bottom of pie crust with berries, arranging them close together. Spoon more glaze over berries.

Add balance of berries, arranging them in a mound. Cover berries with more glaze, using spatula or pie server to smooth the glaze. Decorate edge of pie with whipped cream and chill.

MAKES 6 SERVINGS

Photograph, Page 11

Mrs. Knott's Chicken Dinner Restaurant

Knott's Berry Farm, 8039 Beach Blvd.,
Buena Park, CA 90622;
(714) 827-1776.

Since its humble beginnings as a single-table dining room back in 1934, Mrs. Knott's has grown into a bustling complex of nine dining rooms that can please 1,150 hungry customers at a single seating. Hearty western breakfasts, and daily lunch and dinner featuring Mrs. Knott's renowned chicken, buttermilk biscuits with Knott's Berry Farm preserves, and heavenly boysenberry pie are just the ticket before or after a big day on the Farm, a mesmerizing amusement mecca with 165 rides, shows, and attractions.

MRS. KNOTT'S BOYSENBERRY PIE

Pie Pastry
2 cups all purpose flour
1/2 teaspoon salt
1/2 cup butter, chilled
1/3 cup vegetable shortening, chilled
4 to 7 tablespoons ice water

Pie Filling
1 cup water
13 tablespoons sugar
Pinch of salt
1 tablespoon corn syrup
1 teaspoon lemon juice
3 tablespoons cornstarch
1/4 cup water
1 (16-ounce) bag frozen boysenberries (do not thaw)
2 crusts pie pastry

To make pie pastry: Sift flour and salt together into bowl. Using pastry blender cut in butter and shortening until mixture is the size of small peas. Sprinkle on water, 1 tablespoon at a time, tossing mixture with pastry blender or a fork. When mixture holds together when pinched between thumb and forefinger, stop adding water.

Gather mixture into a ball and turn out onto floured surface. Divide in half, form into 2 balls and roll with floured rolling pin to desired size. Makes 2 single crusts or 1 double crust.

To make pie filling: In large saucepan combine water, sugar, salt, cornsyrup, and lemon juice and bring to a boil. Combine cornstarch and water and blend well. Add to saucepan and stir together. Heat thoroughly. Add frozen boysenberries.

Pour into unbaked 9-inch pie crust. Cover with top crust and seal well around edges. Make several slashes in top to release steam. Bake at 400 degrees F. for 40 minutes or until top is golden brown. Cool on rack.

MAKES 6 SERVINGS

Shadowbrook

1750 Wharf Rd., Capitola, CA 95010;
(408) 475-1511.

Shadowbrook is a fine restaurant and a unique attraction, beautifully packaged together. Nestled in the hillsides overlooking Soquel Creek at Capitola-by-the-Sea, Shadowbrook uses a cable car to whisk its guests from the parking areas. The restaurant itself is a charming Swiss chalet that has been a local landmark since 1947. Delicious prime rib, steaks, and fresh seafoods, are complemented by a broad-based wine list. Guests may dine inside, or al fresco in the garden patio.

CHOCOLATE FUDGE TORTE

Crust
1¼ cups Oreo cookie crumbs
½ cup sifted confectioners' sugar
½ cup butter, melted

Torte
*All ingredients should be room
   temperature*
9 egg yolks
1 cup sifted confectioners' sugar
2 tablespoons rum
2 cups unsalted butter, softened
*1 pound semi-sweet chocolate,
   melted*
½ cup sifted cocoa powder
14 egg whites

Garnish
Grated white chocolate

To make crust: Mix Oreo crumbs and sugar together in bowl. Mix butter into Oreo mixture. Press into 10-inch springform pan lined on the bottom with wax paper. Refrigerate until needed.

To make torte: With hand mixer, mix egg yolks and powdered sugar. Heat mixture in double boiler until lukewarm and all sugar is dissolved. Remove from double boiler and whip at high speed with hand mixer until velvety. Add rum and mix. Set mixture aside.

Beat butter until fluffy. Add cocoa and beat until completely mixed. Add egg yolk mixture and beat until mixed. Pour in melted chocolate and mix at high speed until fluffy. Set mixture aside.

Whip egg whites at high speed until they reach soft peak stage. Turn mixer down to low speed and gradually add chocolate mixture. Scrape sides of bowl to make sure all ingredients are mixed well. Mixture should be soft and slightly fluffy. Pour into pan with cookie crust. Refrigerate for several hours. Release from pan and dust with grated white chocolate.

MAKES 16 SERVINGS

Photograph, Page 9

The Corkscrew
English Beef and Seafood House

11647 San Vicente Blvd., Los Angeles, CA 90049;
(213) 826-5501.

Like the hospitable public houses of 18th and 19th century England, The Corkscrew in Brentwood specializes in generous cuts of prime beef, prepared to succulent perfection. But since this particular pub happens to be modern-day Southern California, it has added some touches peculiar to the region. Fresh California seafoods, imaginative ways with chicken, and bountiful salads and soups share equal billing with the beef.

FATHER'S FAVORITE DESSERT

3 rounded tablespoons butter, melted
1 heaping cup graham cracker crumbs
2 heaping cups sifted confectioners' sugar
1³/₄ cups soft butter
1 teaspoon vanilla extract
Pinch of salt
3 eggs, separated
1 cup thick chocolate sauce (Hershey's fudge)
3 squares melted semi-sweet chocolate
³/₄ cup chopped walnuts

Garnish
Whipped cream
Shaved semi-sweet chocolate

Butter a 9-inch by 12-inch glass dish. With fingers blend the melted butter with about ²/₃ cup of the crumbs and pat onto bottom of pan for crust.

Combine sugar, butter, vanilla, and salt in bowl and mix until well blended. Add egg yolks to mixture and blend, scraping sides of bowl often.

Fold in chocolate sauce, melted chocolate that has been slightly cooled, and walnuts. Blend well with mixer, scraping sides of bowl often.

Beat egg whites until soft peaks form. Fold into chocolate mixture.

Pour into pan and top with remaining crumbs. Stretch plastic wrap across to seal and freeze for 6 to 8 hours.

Before serving place in refrigerator. Cut into squares and top with whipped cream and shaved bittersweet chocolate.

MAKES 12 SERVINGS

Ocean Avenue, Carmel-By-The-Sea, Ca. 93921;
(408) 624-2569

Renowned for its warmth and hospitality, and its succulent oakwood-pit broiling, the Carmel Butcher Shop is an integral part of the charm of old Carmel. With a fireplace glowing in the front window, great drinks, and splendid cooking, the Butcher Shop welcomes you into a cozy setting conducive to good companionship. Some feature attractions include a bountiful two-pound porterhouse, Maine lobster, barbecued ribs, veal, roast duckling, pastas, and salads.

DOUBLE DECKER CHEESE CAKE

Crumb Crust
Butter for coating
Graham cracker crumbs for coating

Cheese Cake
5¹/₂ pounds cream cheese
3 cups sugar
11 eggs
4 egg yolks
Juice of 1 lemon
2 teaspoons vanilla extract
¹/₂ cup raspberry preserves

Whipped Cream Frosting
1 quart heavy cream
1 cup confectioners' sugar
1 teaspoon vanilla extract
¹/₄ teaspoon lemon flavoring

Garnish
Fresh fruit in season

To make crumb crust: Coat the inside of 2 (9-inch) springform pans with butter, covering evenly and entirely. Put in graham cracker crumbs and swirl around until pans are coated. Set aside.

To make cheese cake: In electric mixer, cream cheese and sugar together until fluffy. Add eggs 1 at a time, beating well after each. Add lemon juice and vanilla. Pour into prepared pans. Place pans in a large roasting pan, partially filled with water. Bake at 400 degrees F. for 50 minutes. Allow to cool and remove from pans.

To make whipped cream frosting: Whip cream together with sugar. When partially thick, add vanilla and lemon flavor slowly, and whip to stiff peaks.

Spread top of one cake with raspberry preserves and place second cake on top. Spread cake with whipped cream frosting to cover top and sides. Garnish with fresh fruit in season.

MAKES 16 SERVINGS

Photograph, Page 9

Barragan's Irish Mexican Cafe

827 W. Glenoaks Blvd., Glendale, CA 91202;
(818) 240-3129.

This quaint cafe with the unusual name has been pleasing guests in the west end of the San Fernando Valley for nearly a decade. Under the friendly guiding hand of owners Frank and Yolanda Barragan, the Cafe is a popular lunchtime destination for workers and customers in Glendale's financial and business districts. At dinner, Barragan's is a family tradition, serving their famed Barragan burrito and other Mexican delights in a friendly, relaxed setting.

FRANKIE'S FLAN

1²/₃ cups sugar
4 eggs
4 egg yolks
2 (13-ounce) cans evaporated milk
1 teaspoon vanilla extract

Put 1 cup sugar in 8-inch skillet over high heat. Begin to turn heat down gradually, stirring vigorously. Sugar will begin to melt and turn brown as it caramelizes. Remove from heat and pour into bottom of 8 ovenproof custard cups. Caramel will harden now but melt later when it cooks.

Beat eggs and egg yolks together for 30 seconds. Set aside. In mixing bowl, blend milk, vanilla, and ²/₃ cup sugar. Then combine eggs and milk mixture. Pour mixture into the caramel-coated custard cups.

Place cups in 2-inch deep baking pan half-filled with water. Bake at 325 degrees F. approximately 2 hours. Center of mixture should be firm to the touch before removing from oven.

Refrigerate cups approximately 1 hour before serving. To remove flan from cup, run a sharp knife between flan and cup. Turn upside down onto a serving plate. Caramel will top the flan.

MAKES 8 SERVINGS

The Carnelian Room

Bank of America World Headquarters Bldg.,
555 California St., San Francisco, CA 94104;
(415) 433-7500.

Perhaps the most exclusive dining room in all San Francisco is the Tamalpais, one of 10 private suites in the prestigious Carnelian Room. In this fabulous gem of a room, 52 stories above busy California Street, San Francisco sparkles all around you and your partner. Dine by candlelight, from an extraordinary menu you have personally selected. The evening will be complemented by wines from The Carnelian Room's award-winning list of California and imported vintages.

SOUFFLE CARNAGO

Butter and sugar for mold
2 cups milk
1/2 cup sugar
1/3 cup sifted all purpose flour
1/4 cup Grand Marnier, or any
*   orange liqueur*
1 banana, diced
2 ounces semi-sweet chocolate,
*   diced*
5 eggs, separated
2 egg whites

Butter and sugar 6-cup souffle mold.

In a medium saucepan combine sugar and flour. Heat milk in separate saucepan over medium heat. Pour hot milk into flour mixture, stirring constantly with wire whisk. Place saucepan over medium heat, bring to a boil, stirring with wire whisk until mixture thickens.

Remove pan from heat. Stir in liqueur, banana, and chocolate. Beat in egg yolks.

In large bowl, beat egg whites until they form stiff peaks. Fold one-fourth of the whites into sauce to lighten it, then gently fold in the rest of the whites. Pour into souffle mold.

Bake at 400 degrees F. for 20 minutes for a soft center, 25 minutes for a firm center. Serve immediately.

Note: The chocolate gives the interior of the souffle a slightly brown color, but the reward is in the taste.

MAKES 6 SERVINGS

155 S. Hartz Ave., Danville, CA 94526;
(415) 837-6627.

In many engaging ways, the Danville Hotel Restaurant and Saloon is still faithful to the late 19th century, when it was built as Danville's finest lodging place. A popular destination for local families and out-of-town visitors, this handsome historical landmark has three lovely dining rooms and a saloon, whose brass chandeliers, antiques, and lace curtains give an authentic period feeling. The American and Mexican menu reflects the Danville area's past.

SOPAIPILLAS

1/4 cup water (105 to 115 degrees F.)
1 package dry yeast
3/4 cup milk
1 teaspoon salt
3 1/3 tablespoons sugar
1/4 cup butter
1 egg, lighly beaten
3 1/2 cups flour
1 quart cooking oil
Honey for serving

Place warm water in mixing bowl and add yeast. Let stand until yeast is dissolved, about 5 to 8 minutes.

In saucepan scald milk and add salt, sugar, and butter. Let cool to lukewarm (105 to 115 degrees F.), add to yeast mixture and stir in the egg. Gradually stir 3 cups flour to mixture. When dough becomes too thick to stir, add 1/3 cup flour with your hands.

Knead dough on floured board for 10 to 12 minutes. Place dough in greased bowl, turning to coat all sides. Cover dough with towel and let rise for 1 1/2 hours or until double in size.

Dust board with remaining flour. Roll out dough to 1/4 inch thick and cut into squares 3 1/2 inches by 3 1/2 inches. Cut squares in half from corner to corner making them into triangles.

Place 2 inches of oil in saucepan and heat to 350 degrees F. Add dough triangles to hot oil, a few at a time, turning once when they are puffed and browned on the underside.

Serve warm with honey. We recommend biting the end off and filling them with honey.

MAKES 6 TO 8 SERVINGS

Gulliver's

18482 MacArthur Blvd., Irvine, CA 92705;
(714) 833-8411.
13181 Mindanao Way, Marina del Rey, CA;
(213) 821-8866.

This is a popular prime rib house in California. Three cuts of beef are offered at one price and served by waitresses in the garb of Merry Olde England. The dining room is appropriately British, the walls decorated with prints and pewterware. The dessert table is filled with wondrous kickshaws and confections. Inspired by Jonathan Swift and Gulliver's Travels, Gulliver's is a fun, gustatory trip back into 18th century England.

ENGLISH TRIFLE

Pastry Cream
4 eggs
²/₃ cup cornstarch
2 cups sugar
6¹/₂ cups milk
2 drops yellow food coloring
¹/₂ teaspoon vanilla extract

Trifle
2 cups raspberry preserves
²/₃ cup dark rum
3 cups heavy cream, whipped
1 (10-ounce) sponge cake
¹/₂ cup dark rum
6 cups raspberries, fresh or frozen

Garnish
Whipped cream
Sliced strawberries

To make pastry cream: Combine eggs, cornstarch, and sugar. Mix in electric mixer at slow speed. Set aside.

Combine in saucepan milk, food coloring, and vanilla. Bring to a boil and reduce heat to simmer. Add egg mixture gradually, continously whisking, until smooth. Simmer for 5 minutes. Cover with plastic wrap placed directly on mixture. Store in refrigerator at once. Makes 6 cups of pastry cream.

To make trifle: Coat inside of large serving bowl with ¹/₂ cup preserves. Blend ²/₃ cup rum, whipped cream, and pastry cream, which should be strained before using. Set aside.

Slice cake into 4 horizontal slices. Place one cake slice in bottom of bowl and sprinkle lightly with 2 tablespoons of the rum. Coat cake with ¹/₂ cup of raspberry preserves. Spread ¹/₃ pastry cream mixture over and sprinkle 2 cups raspberries evenly. Repeat layers 2 more times.

Finish top layer with fourth piece of sponge cake. Fill pastry bag with whipped cream and decorate. Garnish with fresh strawberries.

MAKES 12 SERVINGS

Photograph, Page 12

Lawry's The Prime Rib

55 N. La Cienega Blvd., Beverly Hills, CA 90211;
(213) 652-2827.

Long before most Americans ever gave much thought to specialization, Lawry's The Prime Rib was a proud and famous trend-setter. Throughout its honored 45-year lifetime, this landmark Beverly Hills dining place has taken pride in preparing and serving one dish, and one dish only. Stainless steel carts wheeled to the tableside give guests the privilege of selecting their own cut of prime rib, which is then cooked precisely to order by a courteous and highly professional staff.

ENGLISH TRIFLE

1 (4½-ounce) package vanilla
   pudding and pie filling mix
2 cups half and half
2 tablespoons dark rum
2¼ cups heavy cream
3 tablespoons sugar
2 tablespoons red raspberry
   preserves
1 (10-inch) round sponge cake
¼ cup brandy
¼ cup dry sherry
27 strawberries

Combine pudding mix and half and half in saucepan. Cook, stirring constantly over moderate heat until mixture comes to a boil and thickens. Add rum, cover with plastic wrap, and chill.

Whip 1¼ cups cream and 1 tablespoon sugar until stiff. Fold into chilled pudding.

Coat inside of a deep 10-inch bowl with raspberry preserves to within 1 inch of the top. Slice cake horizontally into fourths.

Place top slice, crust side up, in bottom of bowl, curving edges of cake upward. Combine brandy and sherry; sprinkle about 2 tablespoons over cake slice.

Spread ⅓ chilled pudding mixture over cake slice. Repeat procedure 2 additional times.

Arrange 15 strawberries on top layer of pudding. Cover with remaining cake layer, crust side down. Sprinkle with remaining brandy-sherry mixture.

Whip remaining cup cream and 2 tablespoons sugar until stiff. Place whipped cream in pastry bag with fluted tip.

Make 12 mounds of whipped cream around edge of bowl and 3 mounds across diameter. Top each mound with a strawberry.

Chill at least 6 hours. To serve, spoon onto chilled dessert plates.

MAKES 12 SERVINGS

The Cellar

350 N. Harbor Blvd., Fullerton, CA 92632;
(714) 525-5682.

Now celebrating its 14th year, The Cellar is an award winning gourmet restaurant specializing in classical French and other European cuisines, as well as imaginative dishes created by proprietor Louis Schnelli, chef Salvatore Troia, and their staff. The Cellar's decor is rustic, yet elegant and totally romantic, a blend of splashing fountains, fresh flowers, tree ferns, candlelight, fine linens, and table settings. The superb cuisine is complemented by a list of over 400 wines.

GRATIN DES FRUITS AU GRAND MARNIER

1 firm ripe pear, peeled and cored
1 ripe peach, peeled
1 navel or temple orange
1 kiwi, peeled
1 fresh pineapple peeled,
  cored, and quartered
16 strawberries
12 raspberries
6 egg yolks
1/2 cup sugar
1/4 cup Grand Marnier

Cut pear crosswise into small slices. Cut peach into 12 slices. Peel orange and section removing pits and membranes. Work over strainer to save juice. Slice kiwi into 8 slices. Cut 16 thin bite-size pieces of pineapple. (All the pineapple will not be used.)

Arrange the fruits, neatly designed, in a serving dish or 4 individual dishes, putting raspberries into the empty spaces. Place dish on a baking sheet and cook at 350 degrees F. until fruits become warm.

Meanwhile over hot, but not boiling, water beat yolks with electric mixer until well blended. Then add reserved orange juice, sugar, and Grand Marnier. Beat until volume has doubled, about 7 to 10 minutes.

Preheat broiler. Lavishly coat the fruits, except raspberries, with the sauce and brown under broiler. Serve immediately.

MAKES 4 SERVINGS

The Westin St. Francis Hotel, Union Square,
335 Powell St., San Francisco, CA 94102;
(415) 956-7777.

Spectacularly perched atop the 32-story St. Francis Hotel Tower, Victor's is reached via dramatic ascent in a glass-enclosed outside elevator. Once ensconced in this stunning aerie, dinner and Sunday brunch patrons are treated to a panoramic view of the downtown skyline and San Francisco Bay, framed by floor-to-ceiling solar bronze windows that enhance the feeling of luxury and comfort.

AURORA PACIFICA

Orange Sauce
3 cups fresh orange juice
1/2 teaspoon cornstarch mixed with
  1 tablespoon orange juice
1 1/2 ounces Grand Marnier

Pastry Circles
1 pound puff pastry (available
  frozen)
1 egg, lightly beaten with 1
  teaspoon water
Sugar for sprinkling

Marinated Strawberries
12 strawberries
6 tablespoons sugar syrup (see
  Note)
1 ounce Grand Marnier
1 teaspoon lemon juice

Raspberry Sauce
1 cup raspberries
1 teaspoon sugar
Juice of 1/2 lemon

To make orange sauce: Place orange juice in saucepan and boil to reduce by half. Stir in cornstarch mixture and cook until thickened.

Stir in Grand Marnier and strain to remove pulp.

To make pastry circles: Roll puff pastry to 1/8 inch thick. Brush with egg mixture and sprinkle lightly with sugar. Cut into 8 (2 1/2-inch) rounds.

Bake according to package directions and cool. Split rounds in half horizontally and pull out unbaked portion and discard.

To make marinated strawberries: Slice strawberries into even slices. In bowl mix sugar syrup, Grand Marnier, and lemon juice and sprinkle over strawberries. Set aside.

To make raspberry sauce: Mix raspberries, sugar, and lemon juice. Puree in food processor or blender.

Place in saucepan, and bring to a boil. Remove from heat and allow to cool. Strain sauce to remove seeds.

AURORA PACIFICA (Continued)

Ginger Sabayon
9 tablespoons sugar
12 egg yolks
1¾ cups dry champagne
Juice of 2 limes
Grated rind of 1 lime
2 tablespoons grated fresh
   ginger root
1½ tablespoons plain gelatin,
   softened in 2 tablespoons
   cold water
1 cup heavy cream, whipped

Garnish
Fresh mint leaves

To make ginger sabayon: In top of double boiler combine sugar, egg yolks, and champagne. Beat with electric beater over boiling water until mixture is thick and fluffy, about 10 minutes. Remove from heat and continue to beat until mixture is cooled. Add lime juice, rind, and ginger. Place bowl of softened gelatin in saucepan of hot water until gelatin melts. Add melted gelatin quickly to ginger mixture, beating well. Beat in whipped cream and refrigerate.

To assemble: Cover base of 8 dessert plates with orange sauce. Place bottom half of puff pastry in center of plate. Cover with strawberries so that their tips are slightly overlapping. With a teaspoon pour a little of the raspberry sauce in a circle around pastry bottom. With edge of a spoon pull the raspberry sauce decoratively into the orange sauce around the pastry. Place 1 tablespoon of sabayon on strawberries and cover with top circle of dough. Garnish with fresh mint leaves.

Note: To make sugar syrup combine equal parts sugar and water in saucepan. Place over low heat and cook, without stirring, until sugar dissolves. Store covered, in a jar in the refrigerator.

MAKES 8 SERVINGS

Photograph, Page 9

Scott's Seafood Grill

2400 Lombard St., San Francisco, CA 94123;
(415) 563-8988

You'll step back into time when you enter the casual but warm atmosphere of Scott's Seafood. Old San Francisco scenes on the walls, soft lighting, and polished hardwood floors warmed with Oriental rugs evoke the congeniality of a bygone era. Have a quiet business lunch, or join the before-and after-theater crowd at the bar. Feast on the fish sauté or fishermen's stew, but save room for the luscious chocolate mousse torte or raspberry jack. Three locations in the bay area.

RASPBERRY JACK

½ pint fresh raspberries
3 tablespoons triple sec liqueur
1 cup heavy cream
8 scoops rich vanilla ice cream

Place rinsed raspberries on a paper towel to absorb any excess water. Then place in a bowl and add 3 tablespoons triple sec.

Let stand until ready to use but no longer than 1 hour.

Whip cream until stiff.

In 4 individual serving dishes, place 2 scoops of vanilla ice cream. Divide raspberries into 4 portions and add to the ice cream. Then top with whipped cream and serve.

MAKES 4 SERVINGS

El Torito

4221 Dolphin Striker Way, Newport Beach, CA 92660; (714) 833-9740.

El Torito has been creating *picante* Mexican cuisine for more than 30 years. Although authentic Mexican food was little known to most Americans in 1954, Larry J. Cano's recipes quickly caught on in California, then spread deliciously across America. Today, El Torito is the oldest nationwide chain of Sonora-style Mexican eateries, with more than 100 locations in 20 states and 35 locations in southern California. All El Torito dishes are prepared fresh daily, and the margaritas are justifiably famous.

EL TORITO'S DEEP-FRIED ICE CREAM

Egg Wash
6 eggs
2 tablespoons water

Cereal Coating Mix
3/4 cup corn flakes, lightly crushed
6 tablespoons granulated sugar
1 1/2 tablespoons cinnamon

Deep-fried Ice Cream
1 pint chocolate-chip ice cream
Oil for deep-frying

Garnish
Whipped cream
Maraschino cherries

To make egg wash: Beat eggs and add water. Set aside.

To make cereal coating mix: Mix corn flakes, sugar, and cinnamon together and set aside.

To make deep-fried ice cream: Form ice cream into 2-ounce balls. Place on cookie sheet in freezer for 2 hours. Remove ice cream from freezer and dip into egg wash then in cereal, back into egg wash, then back into cereal. Be sure ice cream is covered completely. Refreeze.

Remove ice cream balls from freezer and lower into a deep-fryer and fry at 375 degrees F. for 45 to 60 seconds, long enough to bring the inside to serving temperature. Top with rosette of whipped cream and a cherry.

MAKES 8 SERVINGS

Photograph, Page 11

The Crow's Nest

2218 E. Cliff Dr., Santa Cruz, CA 95062;
(408) 476-4560.

For fine dining with a wonderful seaside ambiance, residents of the Santa Cruz area head for the Crow's Nest at the Yacht Harbor. The classy yet casual environment is tailor-made for lunch or dinner indoors, or outside on the deck. Virtually every table offers a view of the harbor or the bay. A second story lounge overlooks Monterey Bay, and features a variety of nightly entertainment. The catch-of-the-day is likely to be succulent salmon or shark, and other favorites from California's coastal waters.

CAFE MOUSSE

2 egg whites
2 tablespoons Taster's Choice
   instant coffee
1/4 teaspoon salt
4 tablespoons sugar
2 cups heavy cream
1/2 cup sugar
2 teaspoons vanilla extract
1/3 cup sliced almonds

Garnish
Whipped cream
8 chocolate-covered expresso
   coffee beans

With electric mixer beat egg whites until they form soft peaks. Add coffee and salt, gradually beating until almost stiff. Gradually add sugar and beat until stiff and satiny.

While still beating, add cream, sugar, and vanilla. Continue to beat until stiff, about 15 to 20 minutes. Add almonds to mixture.

Spoon into individual dessert glasses and freeze.

Remove from freezer 45 minutes before serving.

Garnish with dollop of whipped cream and a chocolate-covered expresso bean.

MAKES 8 SERVINGS

Photograph, Cover and Page 12

WINES

MATCHING FOOD AND WINE

This guide offers a host of suggestions for basic food categories. As helpful and time-proven as these traditional accompaniments are, they are not shackles. Use them as springboards for launching new ideas of your own.

In the following guide groups of food are matched predominately with groups of wine that are from California, Italy, and France, since those are the leading producers of wines consumed in the U.S.A., followed by Germany and others. If you cook with wine always use good quality wine and serve it with that food.

HORS D'OEUVRES, OYSTERS, ESCARGOTS, PATE, MUSHROOMS. Traditionally served with dry white wines or Brut Champagne; often lightly sweet wines such as Riesling or Chenin Blanc are better choices, especially in hot weather.

> *California*—Brut Champagne, Sauvignon Blanc, Chardonnay, French Colombard, Riesling, Chenin Blanc.
> *Italy*—Frascati, Corvo Bianco, Soave, Trebbiano.
> *France*—Brut Champagne, Sancerre (especially with raw oysters), white Graves, jug white Bordeaux, Pouilly-Fumé, St. Veran.
> *Other*—Johannisberg Riesling from Washington State, Vinho Verde from Portugal, Qualitatswein or Kabinett quality wines from Germany's Mosel or Rhine or Franken regions.

DUCK, QUAIL, GAME BIRDS, TURKEY. Good with light red dry wines.

> *California*—Pinot Noir Burgundy, jug red table wine, Cabernet Sauvignon, Merlot.
> *Italy*—Valpolicella, Chianti, Nebbiolo, Merlot.
> *France*—Medoc red Graves, St. Emillion, Côte de Beaune Villages, red Burgundy Note, simple Rosé' or Beaujolais-Village are best with Thanksgiving feasts which are more vegetable than turkey dinners.

BEEF, LAMB, HEARTY, SPICY VEAL OR CHICKEN OR PASTA, BARBECUE, STRONG CHEESE. Dry red table wines.

> *California*—Cabernet Sauvignon, Merlot, Zinfandel, Barbera, Charbonc, Petite Syrah, Pinot Noir, Burgundy, jug reds.
> *Italy*—Chianti Riserva, Nebbiolo Barolo, Brunello de Montalcino, Gattinara, Bardolino Grignolino, Merlot, Montepulciano de Abruzzo.
> *France*—St. Julien Pauillac, St. Emmon Pomerol, Gevrey-Chambertin, Nuits St. George, Côte de Nuits Villages, Hermitage,Châteauneuf-du-Pape jug red Bordeaux or red Burgundy.
> *Other*—Cabernet Sauvignon from Romania, Bulgaria, South Africa, Australia; South African Pinotage, Australian Shiraz, red Rioja or Catalan from Spain; Marechal Foch, Leon Millot, New York State Burgundy from U.S.A.

LIGHT VEAL, CHICKEN, PORK ROAST, LIGHT SEAFOOD GUMBO. Generally light white wines, either dry or off-dry, or some light reds.

California—Chardonnay, Chablis, Sauvignon Blanc, brut Champagne, Gamay Beaujolais (light red).
Italy—Pinot Bianco, Pinot Grigio, Frascati, Soave.
France—White Bordeaux, Muscadet, Vouvray, Pouilly-Fumé, Chablis, St. Veran.
Other—Qualitatswein or Kabinett quality wines from Germany; Vinho Verde from Portugal; Riesling from Alsace or Romania; white table wine from South Africa.

HEARTY VEAL, CHICKEN, PASTA, MILD CHEESE. Red or white wines with more body and robust flavors.

California—Merlot, Napa Gamay, Barbera, jug reds, Gewurztraminer, Fume Blanc, Chardonnay, jug whites.
Italy—Orvieto Secco, Corvo Blanco, Verdicchio (whites); Valpolicella, Chianti, Bardolino (reds).
France—Beaune, Beaujolais, jug red Bordeaux or Burgundy.
Other—Dry white from Rioja or Catalan regions of Spain; Gewurztraminer from Alsace; Seyval Blanc, Vidal Blanc from U.S.A.

CRAB, LOBSTER, OYSTERS, TROUT, POMPANO, BOILED CRAWFISH. Dry white wines with high acidity or German Mosel wines which are off-dry but have high acidity. For rich fish such as salmon, a light red wine may work well.

California—Dry Riesling, Sauvignon Blanc, Brut Champagne, jug whites
Italy—Pinot Grigio, Frascati, Corvo Bianco, Soave, Trebbiano.
France—Chablis, Pouilly-Fumé, Sancerre, jug white Bordeaux.
Other—German Mosel or Rhein of Qualitatswein or Kabinett quality or Trocken (dry); white table wines from South Africa; Rieslings from Pacific Northwest, U.S.A.

LIGHT PASTA. Light white or red wines depending on power of sauce.

California—Chardonnay, Pinot Noir Blanc, dry Riesling.
Italy—Corvo Bianco, Orvieto Secco.
France—Chablis, Beaujolais.
Other—Seyval Blanc, Vidal Blanc from U.S.A.

HAM. Generally matched with rosé.

California—Grenache Rosé, Cabernet Rosé, Gamay, Rosé or Blanc of Pinot Noir, Gewurztraminer, jug rosé.
France—Tavel Rosé, Anjou Rosé.
Other—Rosé from Italy or Portugal.

SPICY FOOD, INCLUDING SPICY CHINESE, MEXICAN, OR PEPPERY BARBECUE. The powerful peppers and very complex flavors in these dishes can smother the taste of wine, often leaving it thin and bitter. Beer is often the best beverage with these foods, but carefully chosen (and well chilled) wines can work very well. These include Gewurztraminer from Alsace or California, Beaujolais from France or U.S.A., Pinotage from South Africa, young California Chardonnay for seafood, French Colombard from California, and hearty young Cabernet Sauvignon or Zinfandel or Merlot from California (especially when chilled to cellar temperature of about 60 degrees F.).

SOUP. No wine is required, but it is delightful to serve a dry sherry with and in creamed soups. In many French country homes there is a custom of pouring about a spoonful of dry red wine into each person's bowl when their soup is nearly gone. The warmth of the bowl releases the wine's bouquet and makes the last spoonsful of soup taste even better.

DESSERTS. You may prefer a fine sweet wine either simply alone or with your dessert.

> *California*—Sweet Chenin Blanc; sweet Riesling; late harvest wines from grapes such as Riesling. Gewurztraminer, or Zinfandel; Port; Cream Sherry; sparkling Moscato or Chenin Blanc; fruit wines such as Blackberry.
>
> *Italy*—Asti Spumante, Marsala.
>
> *France*—Sauternes, Barsac, sweet Champagne, sparkling Muscat.
>
> *Germany*—Rieslings from the Spatlese, Auslese, Beerenauslese, or Trockenbeerenauslese categories.
>
> *Other*—Portugal's Port; sweet Oloroso or Cream Sherry from Spain; Bual or Malmsey Madiera; Concord or Catawba from New York State.

BOLD EXPERIMENTS. There are trendy new flavor combinations springing up, such as light red wine with fish. Chocolate, long shunned as a wine accompaniment now is being seen served with red Burgundy or Pinot Noir. Sweet wines are considered poor food-companions, yet in the Sauternes and Barsac regions of France, the winemakers serve them with melon as an appetizer, with pate instead of the traditional Champagne-and-pate pairing, and with lamb. German wines are sometimes ignored because of their delicacy and light sweetness, but these wines do very well with fish because of their high acidity, and with light meals and snacks because of their crisp fruity flavors. By all means, experiment and search for new pairings.

DIET WINES. Wines labeled "light" list calorie information; most are around 57 calories per 100 milliliters (about 3.8 ounces). Since alcohol is the main source of wine calories, these wines have low alcohol content (8 to 9%). They also have low or no residual sugar, a further culling of calories. German Trocken wines are low in alcohol but they do not list calorie information. To roughly estimate wine calories, take the percent of alcohol listed on the label, double it to determine "proof" and that is the number of calories per ounce. At 12% alcohol, or 24 proof, a wine has 24 calories per ounce, plus calories from any sweetness. (This formula is not accurate enough for people who must strictly measure sugar intake.)

HOW TO READ THE LABEL

What a label will tell you is who made the wine, where, when, and from what grapes or in what style (such as American winemakers borrowing the French terms Burgundy, Chablis, or Champagne.) The name by which the wine is ultimately called can be either the name of a grape (Cabernet Sauvignon), a place (Napa Valley), a region (Sonoma County), a vineyard (California Cellars), or a name the producer made up as a proprietory name (Classic Red.)

Vintage dates do not certify quality, they only mean the grapes were harvested in that year, and any year can produce a poor, good, or fabulous crop.

HOW COLD IS CHILLED?

It is a national crime that we drink our red wines too warm and white wines too cold. The taste of a warm red wine is not at all refreshing and leaves your mouth feeling like flocked wallpaper. What remorse springs from enduring a glass of white wine so cold it makes your teeth recede, only to discover it has warmed and released its bouquet and flavor just as you take the last sip? If you must err, do so in favor of cold and then warm the wine in the glass. In the refrigerator wine drops about 5 degrees per hour, faster in icy water.

> **DRY RED WINE** should be served at 60 to 65 degrees F.
> **LIGHTER RED WINE AND DRY WHITE WINE:** 55 to 60 degrees F.
> **LIGHTER WHITE WINE, VINTAGE CHAMPAGNE, SWEET SHERRY,**
>   **SAUTERNES:** 50 to 55 degrees F.
> **OTHER CHAMPAGNES AND SPARKLING WINES, DRY SHERRY:** 45
>   to 50 degrees F.

Thermometers are available in some wine stores, wine-making supply shops, or you can get them through a wine accessories company.

HOW MUCH IS ENOUGH?

Wine is a beverage of moderation. A serving of wine is 3 to 4 ounces (100 milliliters). If you are serving a different wine with each course, one bottle can serve 8 people allowing 3 ounces each. Using the same wine throughout the meal, allow one-half to a full bottle of wine per person, depending on their fondness for wine and the length of the dinner.

LEFTOVER WINE

Yes, there will be leftover wine. Give it a second chance, don't pour it out. Recork the bottle, refrigerate, and serve the next day, or use it within a week in a sauce, stew, casserole, or roast. Take advantage of the economy of jug wines by pouring into clean, smaller bottles with screw tops, such as those for club soda, and use over the next few weeks (especially handy when cooking for only one or two people).

Dee Stone
Wine Columnist and Editor,
The Arbor Wine Magazine

BASIC STOCKS & SAUCES

BASIC STOCKS

BEEF STOCK. Place 6 pounds of marrow bones and two short ribs in pot with 4 quarts water. Add 1 cup drained canned tomatoes, 3 large carrots, 4 ribs celery, 1 large onion, 2 sprigs parsley, 1 bay leaf, 1 leek if available, pepper, and salt to taste. Bring to a boil, reduce heat, and simmer for 2 to 3 hours. Strain and cool uncovered. When cool remove all fat that comes to top. Refrigerate or freeze in small containers for use as needed. *MAKES 3 QUARTS.*

CHICKEN STOCK. Place about 4 pounds of chicken parts (backs, wings, and necks will do) in 4 quarts water. Add 2 medium whole onions, 5 ribs celery, 3 large carrots, 1 leek if available, pepper, 1 teaspoon salt (more if desired). Simmer for 2 to 3 hours. Strain and cool uncovered. When cool remove all fat that comes to top. Refrigerate or freeze in small containers for use as needed. *MAKES 3 QUARTS.*

FISH STOCK. Heat 1/4 cup olive oil in pot, saute 1 chopped small onion until golden. Add 1 small clove garlic, 1/4 cup white wine, 2 quarts water, fresh herbs (such as tarragon or thyme), sprig fresh parsley, 1 rib celery, 2 carrots, pinch nutmeg, salt and pepper to taste. Add 1 1/2 pounds fish heads and bones (these are available in any market from the butcher and usually are complimentary) and cook for 45 minutes to 1 hour. Strain through fine cheese-cloth twice to make sure no bones get through. After straining, 1/4 cup butter may be melted in stock for extra richness. Cool uncovered, place in small containers, and refrigerate or freeze for future use. *MAKES 1 1/2 QUARTS.*

VEAL STOCK. Place 4 pounds of veal knuckles or other veal bones and 1 pound beef bone with marrow in large pot with 2 quarts of water. Add 1 small onion, 1 bay leaf, 4 cloves, 3 sprigs parsley, 1 teaspoon thyme, 2 ribs celery with leaves, 2 medium carrots, and salt and pepper to taste. Bring to a boil, reduce heat, and simmer for 2 to 3 hours. Strain, cool covered, and refrigerate or freeze. *MAKES 1 1/2 QUARTS.*

BASIC SAUCES

BECHAMEL SAUCE. *A liquid seasoning for food, also known as white sauce, and probably the most important sauce of all as it is the basis for countless dishes.* Melt 2 tablespoons butter, but do not brown, over moderate heat. Add 2 tablespoons flour and stir until well blended. Use a wooden spoon or wire whisk. Heat 1 cup milk almost to a boil and add all at once to flour and butter, stirring vigorously. It will thicken when it come to a boil. Simmer for about 5 minutes. Add salt and white pepper to taste. *MAKES 1 CUP.*

BROWN SAUCE. *Also called Espagnole Sauce, one of the most versatile of the French basic sauces. May be prepared and frozen.* In a saucepan melt 1/2 cup clarified butter (see Glossary). Saute in the butter 1 chopped carrot and 1 chopped onion. Add 1/2 cup flour and stir making a roux. Cook until it turns a deep brown, but do not burn. Add 4 cups boiling beef stock gradually while stirring, 2 cloves garlic, 1 rib celery, diced, 4 sprigs or parsley, and 2 bay leaves. Cook, stirring often, for about 5 minutes.

Add 2 more cups beef stock. Cook 1 1/2 to 2 hours over low heat until sauce reduces by about one-half. Skim off fat as it is cooking. Add 1/2 cup tomato puree or 1/4 cup tomato paste if desired. *MAKES 3 TO 4 CUPS.*

HOLLANDAISE SAUCE. *A popular sauce, similar to Bearnaise sauce, made from eggs, butter, and lemon juice. A quick version may be made in a blender.* Place 3 egg yolks at room temperature, 2 tablespoons lemon juice at room temperature, 1/4 teaspoon salt, and pinch cayenne in blender. Turn on low speed for 2 seconds.

Heat 1/2 cup butter until bubbling but not brown. Turn blender on low speed and gradually add butter. Blend about 15 seconds or until sauce is thickened and smooth. *MAKES ABOUT 1 CUP.*

WHITE SAUCE. See Béchamel Sauce.

GLOSSARY

ABALONE. *A shellfish native to California waters, with a flattened, slightly spiral shell lined with mother-of-pearl. Abalone meat is used in many favorite California dishes.*

AL DENTE. *"To the teeth," an adjective describing food, usually pastas or rice, that is firm to the bite, in contrast to food cooked until soft throughout.*

ARROWROOT. *A plant whose tuberous roots yield starch; a thickening agent.*

BASES. *Concentrated powders or cubes to be added to chicken, beef, or seafood dishes or to be reconstituted with water to make broths or stocks. Commercially available.*

BLANCH. *To precook an ingredient about 1 minute in a large amount of boiling water.*

BOUILLON. *A clear soup or broth, made from various kinds of meat, where the fat has been removed from the stock. Also available in cubes to be reconstituted.*

BUTTERFLY. *To cut partially through and spread open to increase the surface area of food, e.g. shrimp.*

CAPON. *A male chicken, castrated to enhance its special taste and tenderness.*

CARAMEL COLOR. *A brown substance obtained by heating sugar and used as a coloring and flavoring agent.*

CEPES. *Large mushrooms grown in France and canned for export markets. Cap is six inches or more in diameter and yellowish or reddish in color.*

CHANTERELLE. *French name for small edible yellow mushroom.*

CILANTRO. *A form of flat-leafed parsley with a unique herbal flavor.*

CLARIFIED BUTTER. *Butter that has been gently heated and strained so that the whitish salt deposit is left behind.*

DEGLAZE. *To add liquid to the crusty bits left in a saute pan to dissolve them, usually done over heat. This adds flavor to many dishes.*

DEMI-GLACE. *Sauce made from one cup of glace de viande (see below), added to 2 cups brown sauce, simmered over low heat until reduced by half. It should be of a consistency to "half glaze" or coat food.*

DEVEIN. *Commonly refers to cleaning the small black filament from the back of a fish or prawn either before or after cooking.*

EGG WASH. *A combination of eggs and water, one egg to one tablespoon water, which when brushed on pastry encourages even browning. It can also be used to seal one piece of pastry to another.*

FLAME OR FLAMBE. *To pour warmed alcoholic beverages such as brandy, whiskey, or rum over food to set fire to it for purpose of adding flavor.*

FOLD. *To gently incorporate one food stuff into another without breaking it, particularly egg white which needs to remain frothy. If beaten, rather than folded, the froth would be broken down.*

GLACE DE VIANDE, GLACE DU CANARD. *A concentrated stock obtained by reducing beef or duck broth or stock.*

GLAZE. *A stock that is reduced until it coats the back of a spoon. Also a shiny coating, such as syrup, applied to a food. Also to make a food shiny or glossy by coating it with a glaze or by browning under a broiler in a hot oven.*

JULIENNE. *To cut into small, thin strips, about one-eighth by one-eighth by two-and-a-half inches.*

KITCHEN BOUQUET. *A vegetable-based browning and seasoning sauce.*

MARINATE, MARINADE. *To marinate food in a marinade is to soak food for a period of time in a highly seasoned liquid to impart flavor as well as to tenderize it. A marinade often includes wine, vinegar, olive oil, lemon peel and juice, salt, pepper, bay leaves, onions, thyme, parsley, cloves, garlic, and so forth.*

MEDALLIONS. *Small round or ovals of food, particularly of beef or veal, such as tournedos.*

MONOSODIUM GLUTAMATE. *A flavor enhancer sold under such names as MSG and ACCENT.*

NAP. *To coat a food with a rich white sauce, a procedure which is called napping or glazing.*

PERNOD. *An aromatic French liqueur, available in liquor stores.*

PHYLLO. *A papery-thin pastry used in many Greek and Middle Eastern dishes. Difficult to make, but available in the frozen-food case of many grocery and gourmet stores.*

POACH. *To cook food in water or other liquid that is not actually bubbling at a temperature of 160 to 180 degrees F.*

PRAWNS. *In the United States, large shrimp are often called prawns.*

PUFF PASTRY. *A flaky combination of flour and butter bound with water, is generally available in frozen-food cases of most grocery stores.*

PUREE. *A paste produced by rubbing cooked food through a sieve or strainer.*

REDUCE. *To simmer or boil liquid until quantity is decreased. Usually for purpose of concentrating flavors.*

ROUX. *A mixture of equal parts butter, or other fats, and flour cooked together for varying periods of time depending on its use. It is the thickening agent in sauces. Brown rouxs are achieved by cooking and stirring the roux for half an hour.*

SALSA. *Mexican hot sauce with tomato base and seasonings.*

SEAR. *To brown surface of food quickly at high temperature.*

SCALD. *To pour boiling water over an ingredient placed in a collander so that the water will immediately drain from it.*

SCALLOPINE. *Italian for small, thin pieces of meat (scallop), usually veal or fish, flattened and fried in butter.*

SHRIMP TO COOK. *Shrimp may be peeled and deveined either before or after cooking. Whichever way, shrimp should be placed in salted boiling water and cooked until they begin to turn pink, about 3 to 5 minutes, depending on size. Drain immediately and run cold water over them to stop cooking process.*

SIMMER. *To cook food in water or other liquid that is bubbling gently, about 185 to 200 degrees F.*

SIMPLE SYRUP. *Combine 1 quart water to 2 cups sugar and boil for 5 minutes. May be bottled and kept in the refrigerator.*

SOFT BALL. *Syrup that has reached 234 degrees F. To test for soft ball stage, drop a small quantity of syrup into chilled water. Soft ball stage has been reached when it forms a ball that does not disintegrate but flattens out of its own accord when picked up with the fingers.*

TOFU. *A gelatinous high protein soybean curd available in health food stores and grocery markets.*

TOMALLEY. *The liver of lobster and some other shell fish.*

WATER BATH. *To cook food in a container of water (bain marie) to keep it hot and/or prevent it from drying out during cooking. Produces an even heat.*

WOK. *A multi-faceted cooking pan, traditionally used for Chinese cooking to conserve energy and cook foods quickly. It can be used for steaming, stir frying, deep-fat frying, braising, or stewing.*

EQUIVALENT MEASURES

A few grains, pinch, etc. (dry)	Less than $1/8$ teaspoon
Dash (liquid)	2 or 3 drops
1 tablespoon	3 teaspoons
1 fluid ounce	2 tablespoons or $1/8$ cup
$1/4$ cup	4 tablespoons or 2 fluid ounces
$1/3$ cup	$5 1/3$ tablespoons or $2 2/3$ fluid ounces
$1/2$ cup	8 tablespoons or 4 fluid ounces
$3/4$ cup	12 tablespoons or 6 fluid ounces
1 cup	16 tablespoons or 8 fluid ounces
1 cup (liquid)	$1/2$ pint
1 pint	2 cups (liquid) or 16 fluid ounces
1 quart	2 pints or 32 fluid ounces
1 gallon	4 quarts
1 pound (dry)	16 ounces

INDEX

RESTAURANT INDEX

ORDER FORM

MAIL TO: TRIPLE M COMPANY, P.O. Box 720114, Atlanta, GA 30358.

Please fill in reverse side for your order.
Enclosed is my check or money order made out to the
Triple M Company for $_____. (DO NOT SEND CASH.)

Name_____Phone _____

Address_____

City_____State _____Zip_____

Signature_____

Make sure amount of check matches amount added together on reverse side. Allow approximately 6 to 8 weeks for delivery. Add $3.00 per copy for orders for Canada and $6.00 per copy for orders outside North America.

- -

ORDER FORM

MAIL TO: TRIPLE M COMPANY, P.O. Box 720114, Atlanta, GA 30358.

Please fill in reverse side for your order.
Enclosed is my check or money order made out to the
Triple M Company for $_____. (DO NOT SEND CASH.)

Name_____Phone _____

Address_____

City_____State _____Zip_____

Signature_____

Make sure amount of check matches amount added together on reverse side. Allow approximately 6 to 8 weeks for delivery. Add $3.00 per copy for orders for Canada and $6.00 per copy for orders outside North America.

- -

ORDER FORM

MAIL TO: TRIPLE M COMPANY, P.O. Box 720114, Atlanta, GA 30358.

Please fill in reverse side for your order.
Enclosed is my check or money order made out to the
Triple M Company for $_____. (DO NOT SEND CASH.)

Name_____Phone _____

Address_____

City_____State _____Zip_____

Signature_____

Make sure amount of check matches amount added together on reverse side. Allow approximately 6 to 8 weeks for delivery. Add $3.00 per copy for orders for Canada and $6.00 per copy for orders outside North America.

NO.
_____ CUISINE OF CALIFORNIA — $9.95 $_____

OTHER MARMAC COOKBOOKS:

_____ SOUTHERN COOKING FROM MARY MAC'S
          TEA ROOM (Spiral ☐ Hardcover ☐) — $8.95 $_____
_____ CHEF'S SECRETS FROM GREAT RESTAURANT'S IN
          LOUISIANA (Hardcover) — $13.95 $_____
_____ CHEF'S SECRETS FROM GREAT RESTAURANTS IN
          GEORGIA (Hardcover) — $12.95 $_____

          Add appropriate sales tax if mailed in Georgia. $_____
          Add $1 Postage and handling, per book $_____
          Total amount of check or money order $_____

Fill out both sides of coupon and return to address indicated on reverse side of coupon.

- -

NO.
_____ CUISINE OF CALIFORNIA — $9.95 $_____

OTHER MARMAC COOKBOOKS:

_____ SOUTHERN COOKING FROM MARY MAC'S
          TEA ROOM (Spiral ☐ Hardcover ☐) — $8.95 $_____
_____ CHEF'S SECRETS FROM GREAT RESTAURANT'S IN
          LOUISIANA (Hardcover) — $13.95 $_____
_____ CHEF'S SECRETS FROM GREAT RESTAURANTS IN
          GEORGIA (Hardcover) — $12.95 $_____

          Add appropriate sales tax if mailed in Georgia. $_____
          Add $1 Postage and handling, per book $_____
          Total amount of check or money order $_____

Fill out both sides of coupon and return to address indicated on reverse side of coupon.

- -

NO.
_____ CUISINE OF CALIFORNIA — $9.95 $_____

OTHER MARMAC COOKBOOKS:

_____ SOUTHERN COOKING FROM MARY MAC'S
          TEA ROOM (Spiral ☐ Hardcover ☐) — $8.95 $_____
_____ CHEF'S SECRETS FROM GREAT RESTAURANT'S IN
          LOUISIANA (Hardcover) — $13.95 $_____
_____ CHEF'S SECRETS FROM GREAT RESTAURANTS IN
          GEORGIA (Hardcover) — $12.95 $_____

          Add appropriate sales tax if mailed in Georgia. $_____
          Add $1 Postage and handling, per book $_____
          Total amount of check or money order $_____

Fill out both sides of coupon and return to address indicated on reverse side of coupon.